The Multigenre Research Paper
Voice, Passion, and Discovery in Grades 4–6

Camille A. Allen

Heinemann
Portsmouth, NH

Heinemann

361 Hanover Street
Portsmouth, NH 03801–3912
www.heinemann.com

Offices and agents throughout the world

Library of Congress Cataloging-in-Publication Data
Allen, Camille Ann.
    The multigenre research paper : voice, passion, and discovery in
grades 4–6 / Camille A. Allen.
        p.   cm.
    Includes bibliographical references.
    ISBN: 0-325-00319-X
    1. English language—Composition and exercises—Study and
teaching (Elementary).   2. Report writing—Study and teaching
(Elementary).   3. Creative writing—Study and teaching (Elementary).
4. English language—Style.   5. Literary form.   I. Title.
LB1576 .A6127 2001
372.13′028′1—dc21

                                                          00-054044

Editor: Bill Varner
Production: Vicki Kasabian
Cover design: Joni Doherty
Manufacturing: Deanna Richardson

Printed in the United States of America on acid-free paper
Docutech EB 2009

To those whose lives have been
challenged by cancer

Contents

Foreword

First, you have to believe that the world of writing is larger than expository reports. You have to believe that students develop as thinkers when they write in a variety of genres. You have to believe that students learn best when immersed in self-chosen topics they are passionate about. You have to believe that high expectations and thoughtful teacher support lead to success. A teacher who believes these things is one whose classroom I want my child in.

Camille Allen is such a teacher. In *The Multigenre Research Paper: Voice, Passion, and Discovery,* she reveals a vision of education I wasn't sure was possible. Since 1988 I've taught high school students, undergraduates, and teachers to write multigenre papers. Along comes Camille Allen to show through clear, uncluttered prose how fifth graders can demonstrate their learning in multigenre research papers and creative oral presentations. I took plenty of notes about structuring a classroom and introducing writing strategies that will help me teach my older students.

If you are new to multigenre writing, don't let the word throw you. *Multigenre* simply means "composed of many kinds of writing." Multigenre papers are many-voiced and rhetorically diverse. One paper may combine a play, a fictional scene, an interview, poems of many kinds, a newspaper article, a diary entry. . . . You name the genre, it might show up in a multigenre paper.

A college teacher, Camille is able to write this book about teaching children because she and her methods students at Salve Regina University work with a class of fifth graders as they conduct extensive inquiry and create imaginative multigenre projects grounded in research.

This doesn't happen by accident. Through careful teaching and scaffolding the children are led to develop skills of analysis and synthesis, organization, inquiry, technology, problem solving, reading, writing, listening, and speaking. The content is cross-curricular, the learning skills integrated. Camille leads readers through the logistics of the project: how to get started with multigenre work, how to create a synergistic classroom environment, how to design management systems, how to conduct ongoing assessments of students' work. It's all here. There is no guesswork about how she does the teaching.

And to illustrate multigenre possibilities Camille uses plenty of examples of children's writing. In one paper, for example, a student begins with a fact-filled essay about Dian Fossey, preeminent researcher of mountain gorillas. Later in the paper, imagination kicks in when the girl includes a cinquain she has written that ends with a perfect noun she invents to describe Fossey: Gorrillawoman.

The capping event for everyone involved in the multigenre project is a model for bringing together school, university, and community. The evening is called Multigenre Madness. Camille and her students are joined at the university by the fifth graders, their teachers, parents, and relatives. In eight different classrooms the children present their work in writing, art, and performance. It is an indelibly bright educational moment, one that educators, legislators, and community members ought to take a look at.

Camille Allen knows how to teach. She knows how to motivate through example and high expectations. She knows how to create lessons and strategies to teach complex concepts. She knows how to collaborate and bring people together for celebration of work well done. And she knows how to write so readers are propelled forward to learn more.

A teacher myself now for 25 years, I revel in seeing thoughtful, creative colleagues at work. You'll do some reveling yourself when you read this book. Enter this world of multigenre madness. Know that Emily Dickinson was right: "Much madness is divinest sense."

Tom Romano

Acknowledgments

Writing a book can be a very solitary experience. But friends, colleagues, family members, and students have made the writing of this book anything but, and I would like to thank them.

First, thanks to Don Graves, who faxed, phoned, and e-mailed me throughout the entire first draft of the book. His cheery voice and much-needed advice helped me through the most difficult part of the whole adventure. He is a master and a good friend.

Thanks to Laurie Swistak. She is the fantastic fifth-grade teacher who has opened her classroom to me and my students for the past five years. She is always ready to try new things, and her sense of humor and attitude toward life are uplifting. I value her friendship.

Thanks also to Lesley Faria, Alison Ernest, Jana McHenry, and Landa Patterson, teachers who have worked with their students on multigenre research. They have shared their expertise and so many creative ideas for this book.

I thank Kathy Ryan, the head of Children's Services, and Murry Edwards, the Young Adult librarian, at the Newport Public Library. They are always ready to help both our elementary and our university students. Our university library connection is strong and we appreciate that.

My students and Laurie's students deserve credit for all their hard work and creativity. Their exuberance for multigenre research has made teaching and learning a pleasure for me.

A special mention to my daughter, Rebecca Bogyo. The scores of e-mails I received from her throughout the semester energized and encouraged me to continue to write and to reach my goal.

I am grateful to Sister Therese Antone, president of Salve Regina, who granted me a sabbatical to write this book. I am thankful to members of my department for their untiring support.

Many thanks also to Verizon Foundation, which provided us with a grant to buy multimedia stations for the university and the elementary schools. The company's generosity gave our students access to the technology that was needed for the project.

I'd also like to thank Vicki Kasabian, my production editor, Elizabeth Tripp, my copy editor, and Joni Doherty, who designed the cover. Their expertise and creativity are appreciated.

Finally, I thank Bill Varner, my Heinemann editor. His direct, yet low-key suggestions, sprinkled with humor, made the writing and revision of this book seamless and smooth.

IT'S CONTAGIOUS

1

Why You and Your Kids Will Like Multigenre Research

> I don't write for pleasure. I find it tedious. Research papers . . .
> I hate them. Yuck.

I read these honest words about research papers in the journal of a preservice teacher in a language arts methods course. These feelings probably developed over several years. Many students hate to write, much less tackle research papers. They put in their time, do a lot of copying from encyclopedias, and can't wait to get them over with. Teachers dislike reading them because students regurgitate the information with little analysis or interpretation. It can be a time of drudgery, a perfunctory exercise.

In contrast, I've seen multigenre research papers change students' negative perceptions of research, writing, and oral presentations. When given the chance to select their own topics to research, decide which genres to write in, and determine how they want to present their findings to an audience, students change. They become empowered. They assume ownership of their learning and display pride in showing off their accomplishments. They grow.

I've seen students embroiled in conversations, alter time lines to meet deadlines, and continue to revise pieces to accomplish special effects. They've typed right up to the last minute and still had to add just one more piece. They've decorated backboards, rented costumes, sung songs, and read poetry with style and grace. They've immersed themselves in new ways of knowing and expressed themselves from newfound perspectives. The excitement of writing multigenre research papers and making creative presentations has enhanced our love of literacy, and we are all the richer for it.

Multigenre Research Papers

I had never heard about multigenre research papers before the National Council of Teachers of English (NCTE) conference in the fall of 1995. That's when I met Tom Romano and bought his book *Writing with Passion* (1995). It completely changed the way I wanted future teachers to teach language arts. Tom is a lover of reading and writing and it comes across not only in the way he writes but also through the experiences he's shared with his students. I wanted to get my students emotionally involved with language, like Tom did, so it would enhance their desire to read and write and make them lifelong lovers of literacy and learning.

I thought that if I tried multigenre research papers with my university students, I might make my curriculum more relevant for them as future teachers. By participating in the process, they might also learn to apply their newfound knowledge. I began my exploration with multigenre research papers with my students in the spring of 1996. Among those students were hesitant, even reluctant, writers. As we got deeper into the research, one of my students wrote to me in her journal:

> I never thought I would be so excited to write a research paper. The only dilemma I fear now is my ambition to continuously work on this project overlooking my other studies. I believe I've never had this dilemma prior to taking this course.

I wrote my first multigenre research paper along with those students. We made our presentations and we've never turned back.

Since 1996 my university students and I have gone on to work on multigenre projects weekly with different teachers and children in fourth and fifth grades in public and private elementary schools as well as fifth-grade teachers in middle schools. I have, however, continued to work each year with Laurie Swistak, a fifth-grade teacher in a local elementary school in Newport, Rhode Island. Together we have faced a number of problems and challenges. In this book, I would like to share some of our experiences and our most recent thinking about multigenre research papers and presentations.

The best way I can describe a multigenre paper is to say that each piece in the paper utilizes a different genre, reveals one facet of the topic, and makes its own point. Conventional devices do not connect the pieces in a multi-genre paper, nor are the pieces always in chronological order. The paper is instead a collage of writing and artistic expression with an overarching theme that engulfs and informs the reader.

A multigenre research paper, coupled with a culminating oral presentation, not only allows students to deliver the results of investigations but offers them the freedom to integrate the creative and performing arts. They interpret their findings with passion and emotion.

Both my students and Laurie's have told us that it is difficult to truly understand the concept of a multigenre research paper without seeing a complete one. So, let me share a paper written by Julianne, one of Laurie's fifth graders. Julianne is a tall fifth grader with brown hair and large brown eyes that radiate excitement. She is one of those students who loves school and life. She could best be described as exuberant. When she heard about the project, she was very excited, and with her mom's help she chose the topic of Dian Fossey, the famous gorilla researcher. Julianne's multigenre research paper contains a mini research report, a diary entry, poetry, letters, an interview, a newspaper article, an award, and a piece of fiction.

DIAN FOSSEY
Mini Research Report
by Julianne Forchione

Dian Fossey was born in 1932 to Mr. and Mrs. George Fossey, in San Francisco Fairfax, California. Dian's parents divorced when Dian was six, which was in 1938, because of her father's drinking problem. Then Dian's mother remarried to Richard Price, whom Dian hated, and this was because George Fossey's name was forbidden in the household.

In 1949 Dian Fossey attended Marin Junior College, taking a business course, which she despised. In 1954 she graduated from San Jose State College, with a degree in occupational therapy, which she loved. Then she worked at a children's hospital in Kentucky.

She was inspired to study gorillas by the writings of George B. Schaller, who was an American zoologist. Dian Fossey traveled to Africa for the first time in 1963, to observe the gorillas. During this time she met Dr. Louis Leakey. He was a British paleoanthropologist who encouraged her to undertake a long-term field study of gorillas.

In 1967, Dian Fossey moved to Rwanda, Africa, and she established the Karisoke Research Center in the Parc National Des Volcanoes. Dian created the name Karisoke by combining the names of two volcanoes that the Research Center was nestled in between. The volcanoes were Karisimbi and Visoke.

Dian was not an ordinary researcher in the way that at first she would crouch in the tall stalks staying a distance away, so that she did not get hurt. Later on she did her research by getting close to these "gentle animals," as she called them.

While studying the gorillas in the wild Dian Fossey had many different experiences with mountain gorillas. The first time a gorilla made contact with her was in 1970. This gorilla's name was Peanuts, a male blackback. Dian was lying next to him, she softly put her hand out, and Peanuts gently touched it. Eventually the gorillas became Dian's best friends, but there was one in particular that she loved, Digit. One of the worst things that ever happened was that Digit was killed by a poacher. Dian Fossey reacted to this by waging a public campaign against gorilla poaching.

Dian Fossey obtained her Ph.D. at Cambridge University and in 1980 accepted a position at Cornell University that enabled her to begin writing *Gorillas in the Mist*. This later became a movie about her life and emphasized how she tried to protect the gorillas from poachers. *Gorillas in the Mist* was not the only piece of literature that Dian Fossey wrote. She was the author of several *National Geographic* articles too, one in January 1970, October 1971, and one in April 1981.

In 1985, Dian Fossey was brutally murdered in Rwanda, Africa. She was found in the Continental Divide (or, in the middle) of Africa. This tragic death occurred in the Great Rift Valley. Her body was found in a log cabin, and her death remains a mystery, but the reporters suspected that it was a poacher who killed her. Four days after Dian's death, her funeral was held in Karisoke, Africa, and she was buried in the gorilla graveyard.

Dear Diary,

I have just arrived in Rwanda, Africa. My little tin cabin is nestled in between two mountains, Karisimbi and Visoke. I combined the two names and came up with the Karisoke Research Center.

It's beautiful here. I have been to observe the gorillas twice. They are very interesting creatures. There is one in particular that I like, I named him Digit because two of his fingers are attached together. Digit stares at me and wonders what I am doing here.

The photographer (Ian Gountooliesa) should arrive in three days. It's very hard to understand the African languages, but I'm learning.

I hope that in the next 3 or 4 months I will be able to get closer to the gorillas than I have been in the past two days.

I am planning to study many groups of gorillas and then I will be able to identify different families and how they interact.

Dian

Acrostic Poem on Dian Fossey

Drawing a different opinion upon poachers.
In 1932 Dian Fossey was born to Mr. & Mrs. George Fossey.
After Dian Fossey had studied gorillas for 22 years she was
  murdered.
Now, I am sure that all of the gorillas in Africa admire her.

From her childhood, Dian wanted to go to Africa.
Over the years Dian wrote several National Geographic
   articles.
She was a very brave and daring researcher.
Someday poachers will realize why Dian Fossey protected
   gorillas.
Each and every one of us have formed an opinion on her.
Your spirit will always live on, Dian.

CINQUAIN POEM ON DIAN FOSSEY

Researcher
Famous, proud
Preserving, volunteering, venturing
Studying in the jungles of Rwanda
Gorillawoman

HAIKU POEM ON DIAN FOSSEY

Famous researcher
Preserving the gorillas
She's Dian Fossey

Dear Dr. Leakey,

As you know I have just moved to Rwanda, Africa. But you
don't know that I have established the Karisoke Research Center. That's right, it's in the Parc National Des Volcanoes.

I think that the gorillas of the Great Rift Valley are beginning
to like me! I have finally, after three years, made contact with a
gorilla. I was lying next to him (Peanuts), and I softly put my
hand on a bed of leaves, and he gently touched it.

I am so happy that you chose me to be your researcher, I feel
very excited about what has happened, and what will soon
occur.

Please try to write me back. I want to know what you think
about all of my exciting events!

Sincerely,

(Dr.) Dian Fossey

Dear Dian,

I urge you to be careful out in the Great Rift Valley. You know
after so many years of research on these gorillas, I have learned
that they can be very dangerous, especially the male silverback!

Dian, did the photographer arrive yet? I believe his name is Ian Gountooliesa. You know I think you two will really hit it off, you're very similar.

Well I don't have much to say, but I can say, goodbye, and I hope you write again soon!

Sincerely,

(Dr.) Louis Leakey

Interview with Dian Fossey
20/20 with Barbara Walters

INTERVIEWER Good evening, and welcome to *20/20*. I'm Barbara Walters. Tonight we have a very special show for you with Dian Fossey, a famous gorilla researcher living and working in Rwanda, Africa.

DIAN FOSSEY: Well, good evening, America, I'm very happy I could make it tonight.

INTERVIEWER: Oh, my goodness, how do you do it? Risking your life out in the jungles.

DIAN FOSSEY: I don't know how I did it. I just know that from my childhood I always wanted to do research on gorillas. I didn't have a lot of help and I was scared at times.

INTERVIEWER: Well, who inspired you to study the gorillas, there must have been someone who encouraged you?

DIAN FOSSEY: I was really inspired by the writings of George B. Schaller. But when I first made a trip to Rwanda, Africa, which was in 1963, I met Louis Leakey, who encouraged me to undertake a long-term field study of gorillas.

INTERVIEWER: That's very interesting. You must have been really stunned, after a gorilla first touched you, am I right?

DIAN FOSSEY: Oh, gosh, that's a really tough question. I felt wonderful, I mean I just couldn't believe it. This is something I had been working towards for three years.

INTERVIEWER: What impact does your research have on the human race?

DIAN FOSSEY: Well I guess I really did this to protect the gorillas from poachers. And also to show humans that gorillas are very much like us, and they have a lot of the same habits that we do. These animals were becoming extinct, I mean, imagine if we (humans) became extinct.

INTERVIEWER: That's amazing. You are truly a very good person, wanting to risk your life in the jungles of Rwanda, Africa, to save gorillas.

Dian Fossey gets up slowly and walks off the set.

INTERVIEWER: Hey, where are you going? Was it something I said? Dr. Fossey, would you please come back? Well folks that's our show for tonight, thank you for watching *20/20* with Dian Fossey. We're in touch, so you be in touch.

The tragic death of (gorilla researcher) Dian Fossey
by Robert Reimer

Today Dian Fossey was brutally murdered in Rwanda, Africa, in a cresting point, which was the Continental Divide. This tragic death took place in the Great Rift Valley, she was in a log cabin, and the reporters suspect it was a poacher. Dian Fossey was born in 1932, and today, which is December 26, 1985, she died. Which means that she lived for only 53 years, a very short life. In four days Dian's funeral will be held in Karisoke, which is also in Africa, and she will be buried in the gorilla graveyard. And I'm sure that all of the gorillas in Africa will always remember her, and so will we.

NUMBER ONE PROTECTOR OF THE WILD AWARD

Presented by: Louis Leakey and a few others

Presented to: Dian Fossey

Date: August 19, 1977

Protector of: The Mountain Gorilla

Place: Rwanda, Africa, in the Great Rift Valley

_____   _____

Signature of Dian Fossey   Signature of Louis Leakey

_____   _____   _____

Signature of Digit   Signature of Peanuts   Signature of Simba

THE INTRUDER

Hello, my name is Digit, or at least that is what the strange intruder who has been watching us calls me. She comes every day and examines us. Every time she comes she tries to come closer to us than the last time. One day the strange intruder did not come. All of my friends and I were very worried about her. She is so gentle and kind with us, and I would hate to see her go. Due to her absence I called a gorilla meeting.

One of my friends named Peanuts who lives in another area came to listen to me speak, Peanuts brought some of his friends too. "This intruder has been good to us too," I said to my great relatives. We decided to search the jungles of the Great Rift Valley to find her. We found her in the central part of the jungle using a strange tool to cut down traps. From that day forward, my friends and I realized that she has been trying to protect us all of this time. We will do everything we can to protect the intruder, who has become our friend.

It took Julianne about a month to do her research and write the mini research piece. She submitted it twice to Laurie, who returned it with all kinds of suggestions. Then Julianne's creativity came alive when she wrote the rest of her pieces. She bought fancy papers to use when she printed her report and embellished her writing with artwork.

Julianne had the most fun when it came time for her oral presentation. She loves to get up before an audience. She dressed like Dian Fossey in army pants and carried binoculars and a stuffed baby gorilla. She set up a large poster with scenes of gorillas and a map of Africa. She also placed a diorama with live green plants on a table as a background.

When she presented, her voice projected clearly, and she was relaxed and quite enthusiastic in her role. Then Nancy, a university student who had helped Julianne throughout the semester, joined her. They sat down together and Nancy played the role of Barbara Walters while Julianne became Dian Fossey. They modified the interview that Julianne had written in her paper.

The Power and Value of Multigenre

Although each student who participates in the process has different experiences and learns different things, consistently multigenre projects have helped our students build skills, have extended our curriculum in meaningful ways, and have helped our students value themselves and one another. They have prepared our students for future demands and our students have enjoyed themselves in the process. Let me elaborate on the benefits Laurie's and my students have derived from this long-term project.

Helping Students Build Skills

One of the most powerful reasons to have students do multigenre research papers and presentations is that the process allows students to learn skills in context. Students need strong communication skills to further their education, to attain and prosper in their future jobs, and to function effectively in society. They need to practice their reading, writing, listening, and speaking skills. They also need to learn how to conduct research and figure out where to gain the information they need to solve problems. They need to be able to report the results of that research in a variety of formats and to know which is most appropriate for their intended audience. They need to develop organizational skills that will enable them to keep track of their progress and complete tasks on time. They need to learn how to think both analytically and divergently in order to reach goals, which they set for themselves. They need expertise in working with technology. Lastly, they need to learn both how to work independently and how to work collaboratively with others. When students complete multigenre projects, they learn all of these skills.

Students Learn to Conduct Research. Students learn to select and limit meaningful topics of their choice, not one the teacher has assigned. They question whether they will find enough resources about their topics or if they should change their topics if they become disenchanted with them. They learn to use a K–W–L chart and list all they already know about a topic and what they would like to find out next. They become familiar with the multitude of resources their school, local, and university libraries have to offer and they take advantage of them.

Students Read Often. Students begin by spending three weeks reading poetry, character sketches, and nonfiction pieces that they write and share. When they start their research, they are constantly reading information from the Internet, books, newspapers, and magazines. They often collect more information than they can possibly use in their projects, so they must read analytically to choose the most important facts. They also read one another's work throughout the process and read several of their pieces aloud during their final oral presentations.

Students Write. Students begin with poetry, character sketches, and nonfiction pieces to build their confidence in writing. This also helps them build familiarity with the wide number of genres they can use in their papers. They learn to take notes from information they have highlighted. They also write drafts of all their pieces, which Laurie returns multiple times for revision. In preparation for their oral presentations, they synthesize and reduce their information to key terms, which they write on note cards. During the three-month project, they keep weekly journals in which they correspond with Laurie. Here their writing serves as a means to monitor progress, ask questions, and discuss feelings. At the end of the project students write letters to Laurie and to the university students summarizing what they have learned. Throughout the three months, they learn and apply writing process elements and language conventions.

Students Speak in Small- and Large-Group Settings. Each week students work in small groups with my university students and their peers. They discuss their research and share their writing. When they complete their multigenre papers, they make their first oral presentations before their peers from two other fifth-grade classrooms in their school. Then they present to a larger audience of relatives, teachers, and friends at the university. They practice diligently for these presentations to be sure of their content and timing. Many students view their oral presentations as more important to them than the actual writing of the papers. In their future professions they will probably be called upon more often to present information orally than in writing. It is good that they realize the power of speaking clearly and effectively.

Students Learn to Listen. Throughout the process, Laurie and I call upon the students for their input. They have to listen to one another when they brainstorm possible topics, design rubrics for assessing their papers and their presentations, and practice their speeches. They also listen to one another in small groups and informally over the phone in the evenings when they decide upon genres and share pieces. They realize that for a community of learners to function, they must listen before they can respond in thoughtful ways.

Students Learn to Self-Evaluate. Students monitor their performance through weekly journals in which they reflect upon their progress. Based upon how much they have accomplished throughout the week, they set goals for the next week. They write these on their assignment sheets. They design their own evaluation rubrics for the multigenre papers as well as the oral presentations. Throughout the three-month project, Laurie and I do not assign any grades. Instead, students receive feedback on their writing from my students and from Laurie. This allows them time for lots of experimentation. Working without grades helps build a trusting relationship, encourages risk taking, and gives them the opportunity to evaluate themselves. For those who keep them, process journals chronicle the entire research process with dates and accomplishments. Students are often amazed at how much time they have devoted to their projects.

Students Learn to Use Technology. Although many students have computers at home and are familiar with the use of the Internet, for others, this project is their first exposure to computers. When they come to the university, the fifth graders help one another access the Internet. They learn how to use the online catalog, how to find books in the library, and how to print resources from the Internet. They also learn how to use the word processor to type their reports. Many learn how to use software packages that enable them to print certificates, crossword puzzles, and clip art. They are often very particular about the appearance of their papers and want them to look very professional. At the end of the project, students learn to translate highlights of their papers and presentations into PowerPoint presentations for other students in their school.

Students Develop Thinking and Problem-Solving Skills. Thinking and problem solving begin when students have to choose topics that will sustain their interest for three months. They analyze what they already know about their topics and what they want to find out. They decide what resources will provide them with the information they need. They read critically to decide what among all their research is important. They select the kind of writing that will best represent the results of their research. They think divergently about the best ways they can translate their research into oral presentations that will be informative as well as entertaining. They learn to shift direction when things don't go as they planned. They are pushed to higher levels of thinking.

Students Learn to Think Creatively and Imaginatively. Students sketch, paint, and use computer graphics for their papers and oral presentations. Some dress in costumes, design posters, and perform skits. They make their work come alive.

Students Learn Organizational Skills. Students prepare Resource Notebooks in which they keep models of writing, all their drafts, and all their research notes. They each design a three-month plan and set due dates for their many pieces of writing. They also organize what should be due on a weekly basis and complete an assignment sheet at the end of each session.

Students Learn to Collaborate. Students learn the value of collaboration, a skill that is essential for surviving in the real world. They collaborate with family, friends, classmates, university students, and Laurie and me. They provide one another with models of writing, exchange ideas, and share laughter and good conversations. They are rarely alone in this project. They select topics, write, revise, present, and evaluate in a group setting. They learn to appreciate one another's talents and how fundamentally social the process of literacy is.

Extending the Existing Curriculum

As language arts teachers, we know that many dedicated educators spent years developing the NCTE/IRA Standards for the English language arts. The standards are broad, inclusive, and wise. They, as well as local standards and objectives, guide our planning and instruction each year. We have content to cover and skills to teach. We are accountable to our administrators, school boards, and parents. Above all, we are responsible for our students' learning.

The multigenre research paper and presentation allows children to reach language arts standards and meet objectives. Children view learning from varied angles, create new knowledge, organize thought in different ways, and integrate content knowledge. They ask questions, explore research, read for content, analyze, synthesize, and write to convey meaning.

Although the multigenre research paper helps us attain many of the standards espoused by the NCTE and the IRA, it seems best summed up in the standard that states, "Students use spoken, written, and visual language to accomplish their own purposes (e.g., for learning, enjoyment, persuasion, and the exchange of information)" (NCTE/IRA 1996, 3).

Although the multigenre paper and presentation could be treated as a stand-alone unit, Laurie and I found them to be more meaningful when they are integrated over a long period of time within our language arts curriculum. Throughout the year, Laurie's children read seven to ten pieces of literature. With each piece, they study characterization; problems, events, and solutions; main ideas and supporting details; context clues; connotation/denotation; and inferencing. Laurie uses some of the literature to teach students new vocabulary. When Laurie introduces the multigenre project, the children take Laurie's emphasis upon characterization and use that knowledge to build their multigenre characters. They also apply their knowledge of inferencing when they challenge the readers of their multigenre papers to learn information about their topics through the use of many genres.

Laurie's curriculum stresses writing throughout the year. Children respond to literature in the form of journal entries, creative writing, and reader response. They write stories, developing problems, events, and solutions. They also create books of sense poems and write bio-poems based on characters from some of the books they have read. Their familiarity with journal writing translates directly to the journal entries they write after each Tuesday's work on their multigenre papers. Their introduction to poetry provides the background knowledge to prepare them for the variety of poetic forms they will be introduced to during our first three weeks together.

To help her children develop speaking skills, Laurie videotapes them in October when they retell the events from a children's literature book. They critique themselves at that time. We videotape the children for the second time when they make their oral presentations at the university. Again they watch their videos and realize the growth they have made from October to April.

As a culminating activity for the year, Laurie teaches a newspaper unit. Each child in her class creates his or her own newspaper based upon one of the pieces of literature that the children have shared during the year. Her students use the newspaper models they have in their Resource Notebooks to help them with their writing. This newspaper unit, along with the multigenre papers, gives the children lots of writing practice.

The multigenre papers and presentations are natural extensions of Laurie's curriculum. They give the children the chance to build additional skills and to extend their content knowledge in areas of interest. Although they might start slowly and return to their multigenre papers sporadically at the beginning, as the weeks progress, Laurie's students spend more and more time on their research and writing. They learn to work collaboratively on their multigenre projects on Tuesday mornings at school and they learn to work independently at home during the rest of the week. They learn to balance the demands of the multigenre projects with the rest of their curricular requirements.

Together Laurie and her children build their curriculum. The children begin to understand the rationale for various instructional activities. They see the need to practice different forms of writing and to practice presentation skills. They see that their curriculum has purpose and relevance.

Helping Students Value Themselves and One Another

Students who engage in multigenre projects take pride in their work. They conduct research in conceptual areas they know something about and are interested in. They think about, write about, and become experts on their people or events. They become so involved in their topics that they sometimes lose track of time. They forfeit extracurricular activities and other homework areas to focus on the project. They become very attached to and gain a respect for their topics. Brian researched the Battle of Khe Sanh because he wanted to honor his father, who had served in Vietnam. Christa began by studying Walt Disney but found she had no commitment to him. She decided instead to study her grandmother's emigration from Poland to the United States. Bridgitte studied the life of her uncle Paul, whom she loved like a father. Just as she completed her paper, her uncle passed away. At his wake, Bridgitte shared her writing with his friends and relatives. Paula wrote about her lifelong idol, Martin Luther King Jr. She spread his message to her peers through her passionate writing and skits.

Students discover not only their subjects but how it feels to truly know about something and be recognized for this expertise when they share their knowledge with others. When they get inside their subjects, they also discover their own voices because the different genres pry their way into even the minds of reluctant students who are surprised by this sudden interest.

Learning is as much emotional as it is intellectual, and emotions run high throughout all phases of the project. Students want members of their audience to feel as emotionally involved in their topics as they are. They have learned how it feels to know something well.

In an article from *Educational Leadership*, Sylwester (1994) explains the role emotion plays in learning. "We know emotion is important in education—it drives attention, which in turn drives learning, and memory" (60). It's true they get a vision of what's possible when they engage in passionate, long-term learning. They learn and are motivated by something they love doing.

In addition to feeling proud, when students engage in multigenre projects, they feel challenged. During an interview at the end of the project, Mirta said, "This is the longest I've ever worked on a project. Me and my mom were talking about this. After this, nothing's going to be hard because I've had the experience. The multigenre project took a lot of responsibility to do the work and to bring the work in. It also took a lot of courage to do the oral presentation."

Much of the pride and challenge students derive from this project result from their involvement with their extended community of learners. There is a lot of sharing during the three-month process. Students share ideas with their parents and neighbors. Emma was unsure about her topic on the Holocaust, so she asked members of her synagogue for ideas. Brian asked his older sister to help him with the typing of his paper. Lottie and her dad, an English teacher, shared all her pieces of writing and he pushed her to revise and write better pieces. They share ideas and writing inside and outside of school. They also share ideas, writing, and materials with my students. Since my student Jen and Laurie's student Emma were both studying the Holocaust, Jen gladly shared some of her research notes with Emma. Each week, Laurie's students share their thoughts with Laurie through their journals. They also share all their writing drafts with her. The entire community of friends and family works very hard. When the project is done, students feel good about themselves.

Preparing Students for Future Work

Christina mentioned an important point in her final journal entry.

> I liked our multigenre project so much, it really helped me prepare for 6th grade.

She was not the only one who felt prepared. When her classmates Lottie, Julianne, and Brian became sixth graders, I interviewed them. They echoed Christina's sentiments. They found that the requirements of a research paper assigned to them in sixth grade came nowhere close to the demands placed upon them throughout the multigenre project in fifth grade. They felt a lack of challenge and almost a letdown at their teacher's expectations. Their fifth-grade experience with research, writing, and presenting gave them the knowledge and the confidence to more than face the demands of the sixth grade.

A quote by Scollon and Scollon (1986) captures the essence of what multigenre research is all about.

> Planning is our most frequent defense against the unknown future . . . With a plan we seek to control outcomes, to eliminate change, to eliminate the random and the wild . . . Preparing is different. In preparing we always expect diversity of outcomes. In preparing we enlarge the future in our imagination . . . [and] we seek to make ourselves ready. (94)

It is one thing when we feel we are preparing our students to meet challenges, but it is more important when we hear them speak of their own empowerment.

Generating Fun for All

Students like to write multigenre papers. There is something about the novelty and spontaneity of the process that continues to surprise us. After sharing my ideas for a book about multigenre with my friend Tom Newkirk, he wrote back:

> I also think the concept of "multi-genre" is incredibly rich and, in a powerful way, matches the experience children today have with media. Simply watching my children channel-surf, sampling three soap opera plots concurrently, tells me that their concept of genre is different than mine. (They, of course, are appalled that I will sit through commercials when I could be flipping.)

Children—in fact, most people—today are in tune with a fast-paced society. The ability to switch genres, capture moments of genius, and be creative and spontaneous appeals to almost everyone. It might seem that to interpret research in such a nonstrategic way might produce a chaotic paper. On the contrary, the demands of the multigenre paper push us deeper, to convey our information in the richest and most meaningful way. We stretch to reach our goals, and we have fun doing it.

Students get swept up in the process and spend time in and out of class discovering ways to make their writing and creative arts pieces informative and attractive to their audience. Their engagement reminds me of a statement Howard Gardner made in an interview with Daniel Goleman (1995). He said,

> We should use kids' positive states to draw them into learning in the domains where they can develop competencies. Flow is an internal state that signifies that a kid is engaged in a task that's right . . . you learn best when you have something you care about and you can get pleasure from being engaged in. (94)

I've witnessed this flow with both my students and the elementary children. I've experienced it myself. Multigenre research papers have engaged us all.

Final Reflection

When the multigenre projects are done, Laurie and I feel good. The quality of the final papers and presentations is always rewarding and amazing. We are laughing one minute and in tears the next. Each is unique and all are interesting. Maybe it is the diversity, the freedom of expression, the break with tradition, or the reputation that precedes this assignment that produces better and better experiences each year. It seems that our time together goes by too quickly.

On both the elementary and university levels, by engaging our students in multigenre research, Laurie and I feel we are preparing our students well. To help you prepare for your first attempts with multigenre research, in the following chapters I will explain how to get started, create the classroom environment, design management systems, and conduct initial assessments. I will discuss how we introduce our students to research and how we explore poetry, character sketching, and nonfiction. I will share elementary children's as well as university students' pieces of writing, journal entries, and multigenre papers. I found that no matter what the level, selected excerpts from former students' papers serve as critical teaching tools. I will describe our students' presentations of their work and their parents' comments about the entire project. Finally, I will share our methods of authentic assessment that help us determine the value of the entire project.

It is often difficult to make change and take risks without knowing the outcome of that change. The key is to remain open and flexible and to expect to get better over time. Laurie and I welcome questions and comments from readers of this book before, during, or after you experiment with your first multigenre papers. If you would like to reach us, you can contact us at *allenc@salve.edu* and *lswistak@ride.ri.net.*

If your students don't like to write or even if you as the classroom teacher are not comfortable writing and sharing your writing, the multigenre research paper might be a more interesting and appealing way to introduce more writing, research, and presentation skills into your classroom. Given the choice, we do what we enjoy doing. It is my hope that my future teachers will go on to share their enjoyment for writing and their improved literacy skills with their future students. Let's get started so that you too can share the multigenre research experience with your students.

NUTS AND BOLTS
Getting Started on a Multigenre Project

2

Plant the Seed

It's important to give the children think time before they have to choose topics. About a month before Laurie actually begins the multigenre project, she introduces the idea to her children. She tells them, "In about a month we are going to be starting a new project for which you will be conducting research on a topic of your choice. Your job will be to decide who or what you would like to learn about. It's a big challenge because once you decide, you will be working on that topic for three months."

Laurie's kids get into a discussion right away. They want to know what they are going to be doing and why it's going to take three months. That's a long time for fifth graders to work on anything. Conversations often start off like this:

"Can we do any topic? How about George Washington?" Pete asks.

"Are you interested in learning more about George Washington?" Laurie asks.

"No, not really."

"Then why did you name him?"

"I thought that's what you wanted."

The first step in the multigenre project is to be sure that students select topics of their choice. In most traditional research assignments, teachers assign topics or give students options that they think will extend students' knowledge of the existing curriculum. The desire to please the teacher and to receive good grades also weighs heavily on students' minds. All that has to change. We have to assure students that it's not what the teacher wants, but what the children want to learn or have a need to know more about.

From our experience, Laurie and I have found that the most successful multigenre papers are those that focus on people or events. It is difficult to write in multiple genres from the perspective of a dolphin or a horse. We also have steered away from writing multigenre papers about family members, because in most cases, student research is limited to interviews and reviews of family albums. We want students to learn to conduct research from more varied sources. In the past, however, once students have understood the requirements for a multigenre paper, if they chose topics about which they had a strong passion, we have negotiated with them about animal and family topics.

Laurie's initial discussion with her children is intended to get them to start thinking and to talk about the multigenre project in a casual, no-pressure environment. Then they have a month to share their ideas with their friends, their families, and members of their community. During this month, Laurie discusses topic choice from time to time. In the next chapter on conducting research, I discuss topic selection and ways to help students make choices. You might use some of these ideas to get your students thinking.

Create Resource Notebooks

For one teacher to manage twenty-plus students' independent research, writing, and preparation for oral presentations requires organization. Fifth graders are not noted for their organization or their neatness. From our work over the years, Laurie and I have developed a Resource Notebook that can keep them on track, teach them organizational skills, and help save a teacher's sanity.

Laurie requires each student to purchase a three-ring binder, which he or she will divide into three sections.

Section One

In section one, students place examples of different kinds of writing that they can use as models. They will work with Laurie one day a week on their multigenre projects but will be responsible to work independently, at home, for the rest of the week. It is helpful to have these writing samples at hand. To begin, Laurie orders a newspaper for each of her students and distributes them. She instructs them, "Once you get your paper, work with a partner and make a list of all the types of writing you can find in the newspaper. When you've finished, raise your hands, and we'll brainstorm a list."

They begin immediately. Within a few minutes they are ready and a student volunteers to write at the board. Students call out the sections, "Front Page, Sports, Editorials, Comics, Weather, Food, Entertainment, Advice, Travel, Crossword Puzzle, Advertisements, Police and Fire, Horoscope, Calendar and Local Events, Local and State, Opinion, Television and Radio, Classifieds, Business, and Obituaries."

Laurie has them cut out a sample of each of these and the title of each section, such as Business. Students paste the samples and titles on 8½-by-11-inch white sheets of paper and slip them into plastic sleeves. At this time Laurie also distributes a sample of each of the following types of poetry: ballad, limerick, cinquain, onomatopoeia, acrostic, haiku, and narrative. She also supplies them with definitions and samples of metaphors, similes, and alliteration. They have already discussed these forms of poetry and literary devices earlier in the year. Although the students might choose to write in genres beyond the ones they have compiled in these notebooks, it is good to have these basic models of writing as a review and a quick reference.

Section Two

In the second section of the notebooks, the children keep all the drafts of their writing. In a sense, this section of the notebook serves as a portfolio of their work. Laurie and her students can refer to it periodically throughout the project and again at the end when they want to reflect upon student progress.

Section Three

For the third section Laurie requires her students to purchase a folder with pockets. Here they keep all their research notes and any printouts they get from the Internet. They continue to refer to this section for the information they need to write their genres.

When the students finish organizing their notebooks, Laurie instructs them, "Put your names on these binders and place them on the shelf at the back of the room. They will be available whenever you need them. You can take them home to work on, but you must bring them back on Tuesday mornings, when we will be working on our multigenre research, and again on Wednesday mornings, when we will talk about any of your questions or concerns."

Connect with Parents

Just before our project begins, Laurie sends the first of a series of notes home to parents.

Dear Parents,

Our partnership with Salve Regina University is almost ready to begin. The children will meet their mentors for the first time on Tuesday, January 19. We will work with them every Tuesday thereafter until the end of April, when classes end for the college students.

Every child will choose a topic that he or she would like to write about. Once they begin working they must stay with the topic chosen. We are just beginning the discussion stage for the choosing of topics.

Each child will need a three-ring binder and a folder with two pockets. All research materials will be placed in their folders and their rough drafts will be placed in their notebooks.

All final projects must be typed on the computer. If a child does not have access to a computer at home, I will allow him or her time in school. Nothing is to be done on the computer until handwritten copies have been submitted to me for editing.

Once the children have decided on their topics, I will send a list home. If you have any materials that might be helpful to another child and are willing to send them in, we would appreciate it. Please make sure your name is on them so that we can return all materials.

I have emphasized to my students what an exciting opportunity for learning this will be. It is very important that they do their very best work and that all assignments are turned in on time. Please reinforce this with your child.

If you have any questions, please feel free to call me at school or at home. Soon I will send home a detailed list of what is expected from the children.

Sincerely,

Mrs. Swistak

Much of our multigenre project requires students to complete work on their own outside of class. Parents are a wonderful and necessary support system. Keeping them informed moves the project forward.

Create a Time Line

Laurie and I draft a three-month time line with topics for each week. We begin most sessions with a ten-minute mini-lesson on the topic for the week and then the children work. Although we do not share all the details of the time line with the children, we do give them the dates of our sessions and remind them periodically about when specific items are due. Here's a sample schedule:

Week	*Tasks*
One	Study poetry and song
Two	Study character sketches
Three	Study nonfiction, select topics for research, make K–W–Ls
Four	Elementary school vacation
Five	Visit the university to use computers and multimedia lab for research
Six	Design evaluation criteria/weekly planner Review past multigenre papers
Seven	Study references/conduct writers workshop
Eight	Conduct writers workshop
Nine	Conduct writers workshop
Ten	Work on editing/writers workshop/the creative arts
Eleven	Work on editing/writers workshop/the creative arts
Twelve	Elementary school vacation
Thirteen	Introduce oral presentation skills

Week	*Tasks*	**21**
Fourteen	Practice presentations at elementary school	*Nuts and*
	Hold presentations at the university	*Bolts*

We spend the first three sessions working on poetry, character sketches, and nonfiction writing. Toward the end of the third session, students select topics and complete K–W–Ls. Then the children go on their February vacation. This gives them the chance to finalize their topics and discuss last-minute selections with their parents and friends. When they return they are ready for their trip to the university to conduct their research. From that week forward they are constantly reading, taking notes from the resources they gather, and writing. Students work at different rates and in different ways. We gradually introduce concepts and they accommodate their assignments for the week accordingly.

During our sixth visit we share our time line and the students review what will happen each week. At this time we let them review past multigenre papers from former fifth graders and university students. We also brainstorm criteria they think make a good paper. We devote the following week to recording resources so they will keep their materials organized. Following this mini-lesson, the students continue to take notes and write.

We devote our next two sessions to writing. Students focus first upon writing their required pieces. These requirements vary by the year and are up for negotiation between Laurie and her students. Usually they include a research piece, a newspaper article, a piece of fiction, and some poetry. Then the students are free to interpret their research in any number of creative ways. These will be discussed in future chapters.

Although students are constantly writing and editing, we do dedicate the next two sessions to editing. By this time students have written many pieces and they must be approved by Laurie before they can be typed. Since there are only a few sessions left, we must be sure all students are moving ahead on schedule. During these two sessions we also introduce students to the creative arts and the ways that former students have incorporated art, music, and drama into their papers and presentations.

Students then have another week of vacation. Here is when they usually complete their unfinished work and begin their creative arts pieces. Parents push them along and encourage them because they are at home.

When they return they only have two weeks left. The first week, we introduce them to oral presentation skills so that they can get ready to practice. The second week, we have them practice their speeches in school and then go to the university one evening for their presentations for family and friends.

The diversity of topics your students choose, the level of your children's abilities, and your existing curriculum will probably change both your weekly topics for mini-lessons and your time frame. Depending upon our students' needs, we modify our mini-lessons and requirements each year. That is the beauty of the multigenre research project—it calls for constant problem solving, creativity, and flexibility. Everyone learns together.

In future chapters I discuss each of these topics in detail and provide a variety of mini-lessons. You can decide when or if you will incorporate them into your multigenre research projects. I also include writing samples from both the children and my university students. Although there are some topics that my university students choose that might not be appropriate to share with fifth graders, many former papers of both fifth graders and university students serve as great models for those who are trying to grasp exactly what multigenre research is.

Prepare for Evaluation

Another critical piece that has to be considered from day one is the fact that these multigenre projects must be evaluated and graded. Growth in skills and attitudes must also be measured. I discuss evaluation of the papers and oral presentations in later chapters, but you might want to administer the Literacy Survey (Figure 2–1) to your students during your first day and again at the end of the project.

At the beginning of the semester, Elizabeth, one of my university students, wrote the following in her Literacy Survey:

> Writing is one of my least favorite things. I never write. I do not have confidence in my writing and I get nervous to share with others. I have always hated writing especially big research papers.

LITERACY SURVEY

Name _____ Date _____

1. Are you a writer? If so, what do you write?

2. How do you feel about writing?

3. Are you a reader? If so, what do you read?

4. How do you feel about reading?

5. If you have written a research paper(s), what were some of the topics?

6. How do you feel about writing a research paper?

7. If you could choose any topics to research and write about, what would they be?

FIGURE 2–1.   Literacy Survey

When I administered the Literacy Survey at the end of the semester, Elizabeth had this to say:

> My feeling about writing has changed dramatically. I am a writer. I enjoy it and look forward to getting the time to write. I enjoyed the multigenre paper. It was fun and a new way of writing. I think it is a great way to write a paper.

If I had simply read her multigenre paper and watched her presentation, I would never have known the impact the project had made upon her attitude toward writing. Currently she is teaching in a gifted program in Connecticut. I am pleased to know that she now likes to write. How much better a teacher she will be because of this.

Keep Response Journals

Laurie and I both have our students keep response journals. Laurie starts using response journals in the fall when she wants her students to reflect upon literature that they read. For the multigenre project, Laurie has her children use university blue books—the kind we use for essay exams. At the end of each Tuesday's mini-lesson and workshop time, she asks her students to take their response journals home, complete them as part of their homework, and return them Wednesday morning, when they will discuss questions or concerns. The children are to respond to the following questions:

> What did you accomplish today?
> How do you feel about it?
> What questions do you have at this time?

Emma, a fifth grader who wrote her multigenre paper on Denmark during the Holocaust, wrote the following in her response journal:

> Mrs. Swistak handed back the rough drafts I had handed her yesterday. She said that all were great but my newspaper piece needed a little more information. Also for my wanted poster I could use actual people and pictures. So next my mentor and I worked on my newspaper article. When we finished editing and adding we worked a little bit on the wanted poster, then we worked on the broadcast script. For homework I have to work on the broadcast script, type out some genres, and work on the rough drafts of more genres. After my mentor left, our class went to the library and I looked up the trials for the wanted poster. There were no pictures in the encyclopedia and the info was vague. I feel like I'm doing ok this week. I'm making progress. I don't have any questions at this time.

These weekly response journals help you track student progress even though you might not get to conference with each of your students every week. As a classroom teacher, it would also be a good idea to keep your own response journal. Anecdotal notes about the time spent working with your children on the multigenre papers will help you refine the process and shape future projects.

Consider Process Journals

Another very valuable tool for evaluating student commitment to the project has been process journals. In these journals, my university students keep a chronological record of their research and writing as they prepare their papers and presentations.

One of my students, Jen, who also wrote her multigenre research paper on the Holocaust, began her process journal on February 12:

> Friday 2/12 I spent the entire evening on the Internet. Everyone must have had the same idea because the connecting time was long. I collected hundreds of pages on the Holocaust, several photos, and diary entries. After a few hours I had to stop researching. It became too difficult. I brainstormed ideas for my paper, I wrote them into my planner. I consulted with my sister. So far—I like all of my ideas.

Jen recorded thirty-two entries in her process journal between February 12 and April 26. If she had not kept the process journal, she would not remember all that she accomplished, and I would only see her finished product and presentation. Within her entries she told me she visited the Jewish Community Center and bought and read Elie Weisel's *Night, Denying the Holocaust,* and *The Fifth Son.* She included lists of ideas she brainstormed, genres she was considering, and the fact that she contacted the U.S. Holocaust Memorial Museum in Washington. When she was too busy, her boyfriend went to a public library to pick up some books for her. She watched an interview with a survivor. She even wrote about how dedicated she was to the project: "It's Saturday night and I'm in doing my paper!" She also informed me that she and her father went to the Avon Cinema in Providence to see the film *The Final Days,* a documentary of five Hungarian Holocaust survivors.

When students keep process journals, it gives us insight into how they think. Instead of just receiving the final product, we see how they conducted their research, analyzed their notes, generated their genres, contemplated ways to incorporate the arts, and involved friends and family in their projects.

If you are working with upper elementary or middle school students who you think will have the drive to record not only response journals but also process journals, you will find these records to be some of your most powerful assessment tools. If you decide to use process journals, you must also introduce them at the beginning of the project.

Schedule Computer Use

In the past, Laurie and I scrambled until the last minute to get all the children's papers typed in final form. We now require that the children first handwrite their drafts on lined paper, using every other line, and place them in the second section of their Resource Notebooks. My students conference with the children about their drafts, and then the children submit them to Laurie for proofing. When she approves them, the children are allowed to type them.

Laurie has four computers in her classroom. She also has the use of three computers in the school's library. Those students who do not have computers at home get to use the school computers first. Laurie schedules them for specific times, and she coordinates with other teachers who share her students to allow the children to occasionally leave other classes to type as the project draws to a close. Laurie also meets children before school to get work typed. All work typed at school is kept there on disk.

A Good Start

By talking about the upcoming project and having the children construct their Resource Notebooks, complete the initial Literacy Surveys, and write their first entries in their response journals, you have introduced them to the multigenre project. You've also drafted a rough time line for yourself and thought about the logistics of how you will organize your students' access to available computers. You and your students are organized. You have a good start.

In the next chapter, I discuss ways to help students select topics and prepare to conduct research and describe systems to keep track of their notes and resources. I also talk about methods to help students access the information they seek.

3 CARE ENOUGH TO REALLY SEARCH

Finding Ways into a Topic

> It seems clear to me that if we want students of any age to become one with literacy, we must afford them chances to achieve optimal psychological experience through reading and writing. (Romano 1995, 193)

When I read that I remember thinking, "Yes! That's what I want for my students!" Romano got his idea about optimal psychological experience from the research of Csikszentmihalyi (1990), who explained that an optimal psychological experience provides a person with a sense of discovery through which he gets transported to a new reality. He gets pushed to higher levels of performance and undreamed-of states of consciousness. Csikszentmihalyi refers to this as being in the state of flow.

Many of my students have told me that they feel transformed while they are working on their papers. Carla, who did her paper on an ESL student, wrote in her journal:

> I wish I had more time to devote to it. Those times I worked on it I was so at ease and full of peace.

They are transformed because they have gotten inside their topics. David McCullough (1999), the famous historian, talks about how he gets immersed in books he is writing:

> People often ask me if I'm "working on a book," and I say yes, because that's what they asked, but in fact they've got the wrong preposition. I'm in the book, in the subject, in the time and the place. Whenever I go away for a couple of days, I have to work to put myself back in it, to get back under the spell. (146)

When given the opportunity to choose their own topics, students really do get emotionally involved, into the flow, and under the spell.

When we assign research topics to our children, we have to ask ourselves a number of questions. How much do they already know about the topic we are assigning? Do they have the background knowledge to understand the topic if they should read about it? Do they care enough about the topic to be motivated to complete the assignment? What is the purpose of this assignment? Are we trying to teach our children the research process or are we trying to have them learn specific content or both? Do we assume that children know where to turn to do the research and that they know how to take notes, keep materials organized, and read, analyze, and synthesize information? How much do we expect them to learn from this one assignment?

If our students know little or nothing about the topic we assign *and* they have to tackle the process of researching at the same time, I'm not sure that they can ever really get inside the topic as McCullough describes. There is just too much for them to internalize at one time.

When we allow children to choose their own topics, at least they already know something about their subjects and will understand better what they research and read. If they have a strong desire to know more about something, their motivation will also help them comprehend better. This will allow them to devote more of their energies to the research and thinking processes. There might be some areas or some topics we decide to hold off-limits, but we have to help students make wise choices with which they can feel satisfied. If we do not allow students to choose their own topics, we could deny them the experience of optimal psychological experience—the flow about which Romano speaks.

If students choose topics they like, it will make the multigenre project good. If students choose topics about which they are passionate, it will make the project great.

Topic Choices That Inspire

I have a passion for Italy. I have written four multigenre papers on topics connected with the country. My first paper was about Maria Montessori, who was born in Italy, was Italy's first female doctor, and became a leader in the field of education. The next year I wrote about Italian immigration because some of my great grandparents and my grandfather were born in Italy. The third year I wrote about Andrea Bocelli, the Italian tenor who has become so popular in the United States. My most recent paper was about Italy in general because I was leading an alumni trip to Italy for my university.

Students might not know they have a passion for a topic unless we bring it to their attention. Just like sharing a list of genres with students increases their awareness of the different types of writing from which they can choose, sharing the topics former students have chosen to write about gives current students ideas to contemplate. Here is a list of nearly two hundred topics chosen by fourth and fifth graders in three different schools as well as those chosen by my university students. Over the past four years, some of these topics have been chosen more than once during the same year and others have been chosen again in successive years. I've tried to categorize them for ease of reading, but you will see that many topics could fall under many categories, and we could easily create additional categories.

Historical Events

Alamo
Apollo 13
aftermath of Hiroshima
atomic bomb
Berlin Wall
civil rights movement
Battle of Gettysburg
Battle of Khe Sanh
Blizzard of 1938
Blizzard of 1978
Cold War
D-Day
Declaration of Independence
Denmark in the Holocaust
Desert Storm
discovery of penicillin
Exxon Valdez
Great Depression
Hindenburg

Holocaust
Hurricane Hugo
integration
Irish Potato Famine
Italian immigration
Man's walk on the moon
Oklahoma City bombing
Pearl Harbor
polio vaccine
racism
Roaring '20s
San Francisco earthquake
slavery
space shuttle
Titanic
Underground Railroad
women's suffrage
Woodstock

Musicians

ABBA
Louis Armstrong
The Beatles
Beethoven
Andrea Bocelli
Garth Brooks
Harry Chapin
Elton John
Jerry Garcia

Amy Grant
David Helfgott
Jimi Hendrix
John Lennon
Madonna
Bob Marley
Dave Matthews
Mozart

Stevie Nicks
Queen
Selena
Paul Simon
Frank Sinatra
Lynyrd Skynyrd
Spice Girls
Tina Turner

Artists

Sam Butcher
Mary Cassatt
Leonardo da Vinci
Walt Disney
Filippo Lippi
Michelangelo

Monet
Precious Moments
Rafaello
Norman Rockwell
Titian
Vincent van Gogh

Photographers

Anne Geddes
William Wegman

Directors
Steven Spielberg

Personal Inspirations

Alicia
ambassador to Greece
a friend

Jacques Cousteau
high school coach
Ryan White

Family Members

father
grandfather
grandmother
great grandmother

mother
parents
uncle

Personal Events
anorexia
Antioch
my life
Ogunquit

Sports

Muhammad Ali
America's Cup
Larry Bird
Roger Clemens
Roberto Clemente
John Elway
Lou Gehrig
hockey
Jaromir Jagr
Michael Jordan
Nancy Kerrigan
lacrosse
Tara Lipinski
Vince Lombardi
Mickey Mantle

Joe Namath
Bobby Orr
Michelle Kwan
Sergei Grinkov and Katerina
    Gordeeva
Jackie Robinson
Gabbi Reece
Mary Lou Retton
Babe Ruth
Joan Benoit Samuelson
Barry Sanders
Kelly Slater
John Stockton
Ted Williams

Current Events

Columbine High School
Ennis Cosby
Flight 800
Bill Gates
John Gotti

1998 Olympics
Gulf War
JonBenet Ramsey
whale in Newport

Topics of Interest

abortion
adoption
alcoholism
autism
Barbie
Black Regiment of the Civil
  War
child abuse
chocolate
cloning
clothing
computer chip
dedicated teachers
divorce
dolphins
dyslexia
ESL
F-117
football
Dian Fossey
Jane Goodall
history of the Broadway
  musical

history of the car
history of jazz
history of TV
history of the World Series
Internet
Lincoln Memorial
Microsoft
Native Americans
neuroblastoma
nutrition
poverty
"Price Is Right"/Bob Barker
rape
septuplets
skin cancer
spinal cord injuries
temporal lobe epilepsy
UFOs
Mount Washington
Winnie the Pooh
Vietnam
witchcraft

Historical Figures

Anastasia
Richard Byrd
Brunelleschi
Cleopatra
Copernicus
Princess Diana
Amelia Earhart
Thomas Edison
Albert Einstein
Queen Elizabeth II
King Francis I
Ben Franklin
Galileo
Mahatma Gandhi
JFK Jr.
Joan of Arc
Sir John Hawkwood
Nathan Hale
Helen Keller

Bobby Kennedy
Jackie Kennedy
John Kennedy
Genghis Khan
Martin Luther King Jr.
Queen Lilivokalani
Abe Lincoln
Lorenzo de'Medici
Golda Meir
Machiavelli
Maria Montessori
Issac Newton
Annie Oakley
Sacajawea
Debra Sampson
Colonel Robert Shaw
Mother Teresa
Harriet Tubman
Wright Brothers

Actors	*Writers*
Lucille Ball	Louisa May Alcott
Marilyn Monroe	Maya Angelou
Mary Tyler Moore	Boccaccio
Rosie O'Donnell	Lewis Carroll
Oprah	Dr. Seuss
Leonardo DiCaprio	Shakespeare
James Dean	
Audrey Hepburn	
Adam Sandler	
John Travolta	

Almost without exception, when Laurie and I look at this list, we can remember which of our students chose each of the topics and his or her reason for doing so. Their papers become such a part of them. Even years later, when I hear certain topics mentioned, I remember my former students who wrote about them.

Questions for Students to Consider

Because topic choice is so important, Laurie and I give our students at least a month to decide. While they are thinking, we spend our three weeks on poetry, character sketches, and nonfiction exercises. During this month, we brainstorm some of the following questions with our students:

Whom do I really admire?
Is there someone I would like to know more about?
Is there someone doing a job I would like to do someday?
Who has been in the news lately?
What events in history have I heard about that I'd like to explore?
Have I read a really good book lately? Who wrote that book?
What music do I like to listen to?
What are my friends thinking about researching?
Do any members of my family have any ideas?
What subject do I like the most in school? Is there something connected with it that I could explore?
Of the topics other students have chosen, which ones would I like to learn about?

K–W–Ls

Once our students have chosen potential topics, Laurie and I like them each to complete a K–W–L chart before heading to the library to begin the research. Heather, who chose the impressionist painter Mary Cassatt, created the K-W-L in Figure 3–1. Under the *K* she wrote what she already knew about Mary. Under the *W* she wrote some of the things she thought she would like to know about the painter. When she completed her research she wrote her major findings under the *L* for what she had learned.

K	W	L
She was an artist.	Did she paint pictures other than women and children?	
She was considered an impressionist.	Was she married?	
She was one of the few women impressionists.	Did she have children?	
She was French.	What was it like to be one of the few women impressionists?	
She painted mainly women and children.	Was she accepted by her male contemporaries?	
	What social background did she come from?	
	Was she financially wealthy from family?	

FIGURE 3–1.   Heather's K–W–L chart

As soon as Heather began her research, she found out that some of the things she thought were true really were not. She also found the answers to many of her questions, which generated many more. The fact that she wrote about what she knew helped her focus what she wanted to know and it also helped her define descriptors for her search on the Internet. I discuss descriptors later in the chapter.

Note-Taking System (Resource Notebook)
Students need to learn a note-taking system before they collect their resources. The 8½-by-11-inch sheets that students access and print from the Internet can be easily stored in the pocket folders of the third section of their Resource Notebooks. We have students use highlighters to select facts from these sheets rather than write the facts on cards. However, if they're using books or magazines, where they cannot write directly on the page, a basic note card system works well. Have the student put the name of the author on the top of a 3-by-5-inch note card and if possible read the source, close the book, and then write the information. When she finishes she can look back at the book to see if she has missed any important points. This helps students avoid plagiarism and allows them to have the information in their own words, ready to write in their papers. Be sure they write the page numbers of where they got the information at the bottom of the cards. They should also store these note cards in the pocket folders at the back of their Resource Notebooks.

Recording Resources

Students can easily acquire lots of resources in a short time. They have to realize that as soon as they take ideas or direct quotes from a source, they must record that source to use as a reference. Students need a system to keep track of what resources they use in their papers and they need the system before they start their research. It doesn't matter what format you use, but it is important to stress that the reason we keep records is so that others who want to read more about our topics can find the materials. At times students fail to follow the format completely, but as long as they report their resources in a responsible way, Laurie and I remain somewhat flexible. We give our students the following samples as a guide.

Resources

Books
Angelou, Maya. 1997. *Even the Stars Look Lonesome.* New York: Random House Inc.

Journals
Wixon, Karen. 1983. "Questions About a Test: What You Ask About Is What Children Learn." *The Reading Teacher* 37, no. 3 (December).

Internet
Earhart, Amelia: Life History. http://www.atchinson.org/Amelia/Life hist.html. 2/13/99.

Interviews
Jackson, Mary. March 20, 2000. Topic: My Neighborhood.

Videos
Andrea Bocelli: A Night in Tuscany. 1997. PolyGram Video, a division of PolyGram Records, Inc. New York, NY.

Students keep their sample resource lists in the third section of their Resource Notebooks along with their printouts from the Internet and their note cards.

Connections with Your School and Local Librarians

Once the students have chosen their topics, devised their note-taking schemes, and prepared themselves to file their resources in their notebooks, we set off for the library to begin our research.

Children need to learn that librarians can be their best friends as they try to do a research paper. I've been friendly with Kim, the Children's librarian at the local public library, since I began teaching at the university many years ago. I recently stopped in to see her and her friend, Meg, the Young Adult librarian, to get advice on doing research with children. Kim began,

"You know, it is really best if the classroom teacher can work with us ahead of time. Teachers from across the city send their children to us and they are all scrambling for resources. If we could plan ahead, we could simplify the process."

"We could also get the resources ready in advance," Meg said. "Sometimes we need to send for resources through interlibrary loan from across the state, and that takes time."

"We also like to be able to direct the children to the proper location in the library. We can designate certain areas where resources will be available if we know ahead," Kim said.

"Well what do you recommend that classroom teachers do to make the process easier for everyone?" I asked.

"I've developed a form that classroom teachers can complete and submit to us before students come to the library. I'll give you a copy," Meg said. (See Figure 3–2.)

"It is really helpful if teachers can send clear directions, the goals and objectives, and a time line for the project," Kim said. "Parents should get a copy of that, too. That way we can all work together. Laurie always sends me a list of the topics her fifth graders choose for their multigenre papers."

Meg added, "I use pathfinders to guide students through the various encyclopedias, books, magazines, and the World Wide Web. I give students these papers so they can begin their work independently. Here's one for sixth graders whose teacher let me know they had to write geology reports." (See Figure 3–3.)

Librarians at schools and public libraries can adapt the ideas and forms that Kim and Meg shared with me. Each pathfinder would be specific to the available resources within each library. The key that both Kim and Meg kept stressing was that there needs to be communication ahead of time between teachers and librarians and the more specific that communication, the better.

Connections with Your Local University Library

One day each year, Laurie and I arrange to have her children come to the university library to do their research. We do this for a number of reasons. First, the university has many computer labs. In these labs each computer has direct access to the Internet. We reserve enough computers so that each child has his or her own computer for about an hour. This gives each child a good amount of time to do research.

We also make sure that a university student or reference librarian takes the children on a tour of the library. They make special stops to check the online catalog to see what books are available on their topics.

They also visit our Curriculum Resource Center, where they have access to magazines such as *Cricket* and *Cobblestone* and a wide variety of children's literature books. Many times they can get good information on their topic from a good children's informational book.

To help us help your students, we would appreciate advance notice of major projects and research reports. This information will give us the opportunity to prepare the staff for the help that your students need. Please fax or drop off this assignment form and as much information (such as handouts that you have regarding assignments) to the library.

PROJECT/TOPIC:

DATE ASSIGNED:

DUE DATE: TEACHER:

SCHOOL: GRADE:

COMMENTS:

PLEASE CHECK ANY AND ALL OF THE FOLLOWING THAT APPLY. WE WILL USE THIS STRICTLY FOR OUR PLANNING AND GUIDANCE FOR THE STUDENTS.

_____ This is a major grade for the students.

_____ This is a minor grade for the students.

_____ This is extra credit for the students.

The purpose of the research in this assignment is to

_____ have students follow a thought process.

_____ find an answer.

_____ learn about different research resources.

_____ produce a product.

FIGURE 3–2.   School Assignment Alert

If they should find some books relevant to their topics, Laurie will check them out for her students. Our university provides all interested community teachers with library cards. Laurie takes the books back to her classroom and houses them on a shelf marked "Multigenre Resources." Those materials are for use in school only and cannot leave the classroom. Any materials that parents send in are also housed there. This creates a temporary reference library.

Another reason we like to take the children to the university is that it exposes them to a wonderful resource. Most of the children live within a

Encyclopedias

Several special encyclopedias (encyclopedias that focus on one topic or subject) will help you find information on your broad topic and perhaps your specific geological event.

Remember: Always use the index first.

The Cambridge Encyclopedia of Earth Sciences Non-Fiction/QE 26.2/C351918

The Planet We Live On: Illustrated Encyclopedia of the Earth Sciences Reference Stacks/QE5.P55/Ref.

Books

To find books on your subject, use the online public access computer (the CLAN catalog). The following search strategies are listed from most useful to least useful.

- **Subject Keyword.** Select 5 on the search screen and type in your broad topic—volcanoes, earthquakes, tsunamis, and geysers.
- **Subject Authority.** Select 4 on the search screen. Use Earth Sciences or the type of natural event (volcano, earthquake). Remember, the answers you see are subjects. If you want to see the books, you'll have to go to the next screen (press Enter).
- **Title Keyword.** This will include books that have the keyword that you are searching for in their title. This is not the best way to search since it will bring up fiction books (which aren't good for a science project).

Two important reminders: Even though the book isn't about your particular subject or specific event, check its index for references to your topic. Also, you want nonfiction—not fiction—books for this report.

Magazines

To find magazine articles, you need to use an index. A good index is Ebsco (which you will find in the reference computers). Ebsco includes the full text of many magazine articles as well as citations to articles that are in magazines, which we have here. To use Ebsco, follow these simple directions.

FIGURE 3–3.   Geology Pathfinder

At the library program screen double click on Magazine Index. At the next screen, press Enter to "Select all Databases." Then press Enter 2 more times.

You will see the Search Screen. On the first line of "Type words to look for" enter your broad term (such as volcanoes); on the next line enter your narrow term (such as Mount Etna). Use the down arrow to get to "Search fulltext" and enter Y, so the computer will look for these terms in the text of magazine articles.

The next screen will have the results of your search. You need to remember several things as you look at your results:

- Use the arrows to scroll up or down the screen.
- Use the Subject heading to see if the article is specifically about your subject.
- If the article has "Fulltext Available Press F7," you can read that article on the computer or print it out. Press F7 to read it and then F6 to print it.
- If citation has "We subscribe to this magazine" under it, write down the magazine name, the date, and the page numbers. We'll get the article for you.
- Use Esc to go back to the previous screen.
- When you're done with your search, press Esc until you see "Exit" in the red column on the left. Arrow down to "Exit" and press Enter. This will complete your search.

The World Wide Web
Yahoo!

www.yahoo.com

Arranged by subject, Yahoo! provides you with a quick, easy way to find *relevant* Web sites on your topic. Follow the path below from the homepage to find some useful material.

Science

    To *Ask an Expert*

        To *Earth Sciences*

            To *Ask a . . . Hurricane Hunter*

                . . . Volcanologist

                . . . Earth Scientist

FIGURE 3–3.   *Continued*

To *Earth Sciences*

To *Geology and Geophysics*

To *Volcanology*

To *Oceanography*

To *Tsunamis*

Also, you can narrow your search within any of these Yahoo! Categories by typing your specific natural event (Mount St. Helen's, for example) in the search box on the screen.

Don't forget: ask a librarian if you need help!

FIGURE 3–3.   *Continued*

few miles of the university, and once they become familiar with its layout and advantages, they can come back anytime, especially during the summer when they are not in school.

A last reason we like to bring them on a field trip is that they get to see life at the university. It inspires them to want to come to college themselves one day.

If you have a college or university nearby, you could probably arrange a field trip there. Contact the reference librarian and see what kind of tour she could provide. With enough notice you can probably arrange to use the computer lab for an hour with several lab technicians who would be able to assist your students in their Internet searches. If you send in your students' topics ahead of time, the reference librarian can make special provisions to meet the needs of your students. It would be good to include parents in the field trip, too. They can help guide the children and learn about the library at the same time.

Research Beyond the Libraries
Internet

The Internet is probably the most up-to-date resource we have today for conducting research. Often when a news event takes place, the results will be posted immediately on the Web. We don't have to wait until the newspaper arrives the next morning. Also, sites that we reach via the Web usually tell us when that site has been most recently updated.

Ron Owston's book *Making the Link* (1998) is an excellent resource for teachers who want to learn the basics about the Internet. He warns, however, that everything we find on the Internet has not passed through the editorial process, so we have no idea who or what organization posted the material. We have to make students aware that what they find on the Internet might not be true. Owston gives in-depth descriptions of the many avenues into the Internet, but probably AltaVista and Yahoo! (Yahooligans) are two that will get most students what they need.

AltaVista (*http://altavista.digital.com*) is one of the largest databases of Web documents. It indexes all the words on each page of all its documents. It can locate a very obscure document and it will produce a very large number of hits. To narrow this number and get more specific, you will need to input descriptors. If we return to Heather's K–W–L and assume she wanted to write her paper on the impressionist painter Mary Cassatt, she could start with "impressionist painters" to get general information. To search the AltaVista database, she should enter the two descriptors in the following way: +impressionist+painters. This would bring up many documents in which those terms appear. If she wanted to reduce the number, she could enter the descriptors +impressionist+painters+ cassatt. For the most direct information, she would enter "mary cassatt." To ensure that she gets to the greatest number of documents on Mary Cassatt in the database, she must place the descriptors in quotation marks and use all lowercase letters. This way AltaVista will read both names together and will not return documents where the first or last names occur independently.

Unlike AltaVista, which is a database of Web documents, Yahoo! (*http://www.yahoo.com*) organizes all Web resources into a directory, which links you to other Web sites. With Yahoo you must start with more general headings like "arts" and then break them down into narrower topics such as "Impressionist painters." Yahooligans is a Web site for children. It has wonderfully clear information and photos that children can use for their papers.

Amazon.com (*http://www.amazon.com*) is also a great resource on the Internet. This site can put students in touch with a number of books and videos related to their topics. Here they can read about these resources and comments made by people who have already purchased them. Students can then look for these books and videos at their local libraries or through interlibrary loans. Also, if a student has lost a reference to a book she has used in her paper, she can usually type in the title and Amazon.com will supply the author, publisher, and publication date.

Videos

Everyone watches videos. They are a part of our culture. Both the fifth graders and my students have made extensive use of videos to complete their research. Julianne, who did her research on Dian Fossey, watched *Gorillas in the Mist* as part of her research. Others have watched *What's Love Got to Do with It?* for research on Tina Turner, *A Hard Day's Night* to learn about the Beatles, and *Titanic* for research on the famous ship. Videos inform students about the characters and help them visualize settings and circumstances. They can inspire a number of forms of writing.

Interviews

For some multigenre papers, interviews are essential. Marcie did her research on skin cancer. She interviewed her mother, who had had skin cancer and surgery to remove it. She even brought her mother to class when she gave her oral presentation and interviewed her before her classmates.

Lisa wanted to focus upon nutrition. She loved to cook and also collected recipes. As part of her research she interviewed the nutritionist at the local hospital. In another instance Kim interviewed her mother about Frank Sinatra. Her mother had gone to see one of his concerts. Kim wrote up the questions and answers in her paper.

In her book *Classroom Interviews* (1998), Paula Rogovin gives wonderful information about strategies for interviewing and also discusses the importance and power of the interview in a child's development. "An interview is a gift—the gift of one's cultural identity and the gift of self-esteem" (23).

Although Laurie and I usually don't allow students to choose family members for topics, if approved, students must interview people to collect information. Christa studied her grandmother who emigrated from Poland. As part of her research, she interviewed in person, by phone, and by letter a number of her family members. Her paper not only informed us about Ellis Island and all that her grandmother endured but also helped Christa better understand her heritage and how she became the person she is.

Primary Sources

It is most powerful if students can get access to primary sources. My student Maria worked in a group home for teenage girls. As part of her research she interviewed the girls and had them discuss their opinions about various topics. Maria played the tape when she gave her oral presentation. It was particularly effective because it brought the girls' voices into the classroom.

Nathan did his research on a family friend who was a diplomat in a foreign country. He was allowed to see family albums and military scrapbooks, read letters between family members, and examine military uniforms from Vietnam. He even saw the flag that was presented at the man's funeral. These items not only gave Nathan information but also inspired many of his pieces of writing.

On-Site Visits

See for yourself! One year we had a fifth grader who was interested in witchcraft. Gail and her mom took a trip to Salem, Massachusetts, to see where the witch trials took place. Amy wrote her multigenre paper on chocolate. She made an appointment to go behind the scenes at a local candy store. The owners allowed her to videotape the whole process of making chocolate and ask any questions she wanted.

Another Amy wrote about Jackie Kennedy. Hammersmith Farm, where Jackie spent many of her summers, is located very near our university.

Amy was able to arrange a private tour and gained a real sense of the type of lifestyle that Jackie lived.

Christa, who wrote her paper on her grandmother from Poland, went with her mother to Ellis Island and the Statue of Liberty. She took lots of photos, including one of the plaque at Ellis Island that listed her grandmother's name. These on-site visits make students real investigators.

When Andrea was young she had neuroblastoma, a form of childhood cancer. She wanted to conduct research about the disease. As part of this research she returned to the hospital where she used to go for treatments. She videotaped her visit and shared that with us during her oral presentation at the end of the semester. It was an emotional and important journey for Andrea.

The Research Piece

Multigenre research papers are primarily that: research papers. We want children to learn the skills to conduct good research and to acquire the desire to continue using these skills for the rest of their lives. Children have a natural curiosity and enjoy searching for facts about their topics. They also enjoy the fact that they can express what they have learned in multiple ways. Laurie requires that one of these ways be a research piece.

The research piece is a two- to four-page expository piece that synthesizes the major facts culled from all the children's reading. It makes the children analyze and synthesize all the research they have collected. If placed at the beginning of their papers, it provides background information for the readers, which helps them understand the many genres that follow. It also serves as the basis for the oral presentations that students must make at the end of the project. Finally, it is a lengthy piece, much like the traditional research papers they will be required to do as they move through the grades. It is the most difficult and the most time-consuming piece for the children. They often feel that once they have accomplished their research piece, the rest of the paper falls into place.

In the following three chapters I will discuss the major mini-lessons and ideas about poetry, character sketches, and nonfiction that Laurie and I share with the children to prepare them to write the rest of their papers. Let's move on to some poetic surprises.

4 POETIC SURPRISES
Easing into Writing

> There are many times when I've felt that there was no poetry inside me, that I had nothing valuable to say. That the real writers were other people. It has taken me a while to believe that the way I feel each day, and the way I and others speak when we're least self-conscious, is where writing comes from. When we begin to speak in the language that is ours and tell our own stories and truths, we are surprised that this too is poetry. (Heard 1995, 9)

If Georgia Heard, an accomplished poet, felt that there was no poetry inside her and that others were the real writers, it is understandable that the rest of us might feel less than confident in our ability to write, much less create poetry. Unpleasant writing experiences have molded our self-expectations. Sadie, one of my students, wrote this about her feeling toward poetry:

> Throughout most of my school career, poetry neither interested me nor moved me. Teachers seemed to introduce it briefly and give a few examples of well known, but at the same time, confusing poetry. We were expected to analyze and pick these apart to try to understand them to the best of our ability. What fun was that? It was meaningless and didn't give any creative opportunities.

Who among us feels we are great poets? More than likely we feel more like Sadie, more like beginners. So that's where we begin, at the beginning. Poetry builds community because it is the great equalizer.

A critical component for a multigenre research paper to be successful is for all involved to feel comfortable with writing and with sharing their writing. If you have reluctant writers in your classroom or if you as a teacher are a reluctant writer, poetry is a good place to ease into writing. It involves short pieces of writing, it can be revised quickly, and it requires few mechanics. Take it one step at a time along with your students. Begin today with some of the following poetry mini-lessons. At the beginning, you and your students might not feel at all confident, but if you share your drafts and fears with one another, you will grow together as a community and will appreciate one another's efforts and honesty. I have been humbled many times by the superior writing and creativity of my students.

Before I get started, I would like to remind you that when you and your students try any of the mini-lessons in this and the following two chapters, it would be good to make photocopies of any pieces that you think could serve as models for future lessons. I often make copies of entire multigenre papers, but I also copy individual samples that I think illustrate specific points from a number of other papers. I place these samples in a notebook, which then can be used as a reference for students.

Within this and the following two chapters I am going to include writing samples from the elementary children, my university students, and me. I include the university students' samples and my own because I share many of them with the fifth graders. Also, I have found that my university students and I need to see pieces written by our peers to be able to define multigenre research papers on our own terms. It will be helpful for you as a teacher to see writing samples written by my students and me to get ideas for your own writing.

Playful Poetics

Share Poems and Songs

The easiest lesson to begin with is to share what already exists. If you have a favorite poem, share it with your students. Ask them if they have any favorites, and if so, to bring them to school. Sometimes they will say they hate poetry and never read it. In that case, ask them what songs they like. Ask them to share the lyrics. Some children who don't like poetry absolutely love music, play it constantly, and will know all the lyrics by heart.

Working in small groups, my students and the children share song titles and lyrics, which they have photocopied or downloaded from the Internet. I once overheard this conversation:

"What song did you choose?" John asked.

"I brought in 'YMCA.' It's an old song, but I love it. When my mom asks me to clean my room I blast the music and I get energized," Dave said.

"My Heart Will Go On" by Celine Dion, "Born to Run" by Bruce Springsteen, "Forever Young" by Bob Dylan, and "Scenes from an Italian Restaurant" by Billy Joel have all been tossed around for comment.

Some share poetry. My students have brought in "Phenomenal Woman" by Maya Angelou, "I Went to the Woods" by Henry David Thoreau, "Lazy Jane" by Shel Silverstein, and "The Road Not Taken" by Robert Frost. The children read poems from books they have brought in. The room erupts with students reading aloud, humming tunes, and laughing. When the children read their favorite poems with confidence and enthusiasm, they surprise my students with how much they know about poetry and how much they enjoy it. Poetry and song evoke emotions quickly and are often enjoyed because of the way they uplift spirits, transcend the ordinary, or comfort readers in ways that let readers identify with the authors.

One year we had a child who loved Lewis Carroll so much she selected him for the topic of her multigenre paper. I would often overhear her quoting his poetry by heart as she conducted research on the Internet or illustrated one of her pieces of writing. Our students' choices of poetry and song reveal their personalities and interests. They are windows to their souls.

Existing poetry serves as a model for students' writing, and once the children have selected their topics, copies of poems inserted into their papers can enhance the mood or extend their information. When they make their oral presentations at the end of the multigenre project, they might also consider quoting lines from appropriate poems.

Share Students' Poetry

Some of our students enjoy poetry and write their own poems in diaries or journals. With some coaxing, you can usually get students to read some of their creations aloud. Although embarrassed, my student Lisa shared a poem she had written when she was in the fifth grade.

GRAMPY

You mean so much,
I miss you so,
I wanted to tell you
I love you so.

After all, I was there
when you died,
a piece of me left
when I ran to my room and cried.

It was all so sudden,
all so brief,
With every day that passes,
My heart is full of grief.

I wish you were with me,
I long for your embrace
My only memory of you
is your face, only your face.

Although the years have passed
I will never forget you.

When I hear your voice
I always ask who
My answer is Grampy

When I stop believing
My heart will come to a stop too!
And I know one day I will see you again.

Although she admits her poem is far from perfect, it displayed her love for her grandfather, and that transcended its imperfections. Her classmates were not as interested in her poetic ability as they were in the emotions and feelings that pushed her to express herself in a way that she could not with narrative. Comments from her classmates made her feel good about her attempt at poetry. Peer support encourages more risk taking.

Create Acrostic Introductions

In our introductory session on poetry, we also get to know one another by playing with acrostic poems about ourselves. Travis, a fifth grader, wrote:

T Tacos are my favorite food because I
R Really like what's in them
A Also playing the
V Viola which
I Is a string instrument. But
S Science is my favorite subject.

Peter, a fifth grader, and Nathan, a preservice teacher, sat side by side and shared facts about themselves.

Popular	**N**onviolent
Energetic	**A**thlete
Talkative	**T**all
Elusive	**H**appy
Red Sox fan	**A**wesome
	November 14

Write "I Am a Person" Poems

In his book *Explore Poetry* (1992), Don Graves introduces us to the poetry starters "I am a person," "I am the one who" and "I am." These are good to try in your first poetry lesson with students because they are easy for students to generate. Students write from experience. Once a student starts researching and gathering information about a person, he or she can write one of these poems from that person's perspective. Here is Heather's first "I am a person" poem:

I AM A PERSON

I am in 5th grade
I am artistic
I am Heather
I am mischievous
I am realistic

I am young
I am originally from Nevada
I am a sister
I am a soccer player
I am a skater
I am talkative
I am unique
I am original
I am blunt

Write List Poems

Again, in *Explore Poetry* (1992), Don Graves introduces readers to the list or column poem. Using this format, a writer can convey a lot of information in a simple way. Having students make a simple list of ideas about themselves helps them realize the number of characteristics and quirks a person can possess. Students often find creative ways to incorporate list poems into their multigenre papers. Kate, a university student, wrote the following list poem.

ME

mess maker
steady thinker
letter writer
cookie baker
risk taker
overachiever
popcorn popper
day dreamer
coffee drinker
problem solver
telephone user
romance reader
dish washer
Geo driver
plant killer
employment seeker
spaghetti boiler
weight lifter
fish caretaker
soap follower
game player
doodle drawer
greeting card sender
shoe buyer
chili consumer
slow typer
listmaker

speed walker
channel switcher
friendly listener
chocolate obsesser
hopeful planner
Spanish translator
cow lover

Play with Language and Art

Currently, I am trying to teach myself to draw by reading a book called *Drawing on the Right Side of the Brain*. Its author, Betty Edwards (1999), explains that the mode of the left side of the brain is verbal and analytical while the right side is global and nonverbal. Edwards argues that we must develop the right side and learn to view things in a different way if we are to learn to draw. Complementing our poetry with art helps us consider how we might extend the impact of our writing through the arts. It also helps us see things in different ways.

Kate plays with language, color, and art in the following poem.

O uthouses
R eally
A re
N asty
G ross
E stablishments

Of course, her drawing was bright orange.

Experiment with Shape Poems

Young children often begin to write by drawing. I've seen many multigenre papers in which students begin with artwork and then complement it with their writing. In a paper about Jaromir Jagr, a famous hockey player, Jessica wrote her poem within a drawing of a hockey puck. Sandra wrote her poem about Paul Simon around the outline of a guitar.

Having students share poetry and song; play with acrostic, list, and "I am a person" poems; and integrate art with their writing gives them the chance to begin writing in nonthreatening ways. It opens up different ways for them to think about themselves and consider the questions they might want to ask themselves about the people or topics they are considering for research. Many of these playful experiments translate nicely into pieces for students' multigenre papers.

Thoughtful Reflections

Georgia Heard said, "Poetry has the power to change us, by helping us sift through the layers of our lives in search of our own truths and our own poems" (1999, 118). Many times students choose very serious topics like the Holocaust, the shootings at Columbine High School, or D-Day for their multigenre papers. They reflect a lot about the tragedy of the events and about their feelings. Although this truthful search can be expressed in some of the formats presented at the beginning of this chapter, they are often best expressed through the use of free verse. Following are some mini-lessons that will encourage students to move in this direction.

Six-Room Poems

One exercise that bolsters students' confidence in their ability to write free verse is the six-room image poem that Georgia Heard describes in *Awakening the Heart* (1999). I used this format in my most recent multigenre paper on Italy. I looked at a photo of Venice as my inspiration. Here is how I wrote my first draft. (I eventually revised it for my paper.)

Heard asks students to divide a piece of paper into six boxes, then look at an image to inspire writing. In the first box, or "room," they should describe something outside that they find amazing, beautiful, or interesting. I wrote:

> *Room 1*
> ancient bricks
> ochre stucco
> sienna plaster
> white marble windowsills
> small window boxes with geraniums
> lacey silver green sage
> dark green shutters
> still dark green canals
> peeling stucco
> bobbing gondolas

In room 2, students must look at the same scene but concentrate upon the quality of light that they see. I wrote:

> *Room 2*
> pale morning light
> foggy

In room 3, students once again focus upon the same image but this time direct their attention to the sounds they hear. I wrote:

> *Room 3*
> gurgle
> swirl
> murmur

The fourth room requires students to write down any questions they might have about the scene they have been describing. I wrote:

Room 4
Who has lived here?
How many generations?
How many births, deaths?
How many family secrets, celebrations?
How long can Venice survive?

In room 5, students have to write about the feelings they have when they look at this image. I wrote:

Room 5
admiration
sadness
hate to see her die

Finally, in room 6, students finish their poems by repeating one word, phrase, or line that they feel is worth repeating. I wrote:

Room 6
Drowning a slow death

From those six rooms I constructed the following first draft of a poem:

VENEZIA

Room 1 Tiny ancient bricks
peak through ochre and sienna sun-baked facades
that have shed their skin under years of pollution

Smooth, white marble windowsills support
small pots of red, cascading geraniums
laced with silver green sage

Room 2 Dark blue-green still canals
swirl into open doorways
gurgling through strings of moss and mold

Room 3 Pale morning light
touches the cobblestone bridges
warming their arched backs

Room 4 What secrets and celebrations has she known?
How many more generations can she tolerate?
How long will she survive?

Room 5 I admire her history
her art and heritage
I hate to see her die

Room 6   She drowns a slow death
                          She drowns a slow death
                          She drowns a slow death

Using this format, Claudia, a fifth grader, wrote the following six-room poem about Sacajawea, the Indian woman who accompanied Lewis and Clark on their expedition.

Forests were dark and spooky
Streams babbling
Rivers rushing
Beautiful sunsets and
Harsh weather

The nights were dark and gloomy
The days were bright from the sun
Dusk came too soon

I can hear the animals howling, sends a chill down my back
The streams are babbling underneath the canoe
The wind is whistling in my ears
I hear birds singing love songs

Where are we going?
How long will it be?
Will we meet any Indians?

I feel scared and
Anxious and
Excited about the journey

Scared
Scared
Scared

Six-room poems are quick but very rewarding. They draw students away from writing silly ditties or poems with contrived rhyming schemes that often destroy what they really want to say.

Stream of Consciousness to Verse

Once your students have completed their research and are familiar with their topics, give them three to five minutes to freewrite in journals all the facts and feelings they have generated while conducting their research. Be sure they are not concerned with grammar, spelling, or mechanics. They are to simply get it all down as quickly as possible. Since they will not be referring to their notes, they will probably record those facts from their research that made the most lasting impression upon them. Their responses to these events will also surface. Next, have them read through these quickwrites and cross out any facts they don't want to put into their poems. Finally, have them each make a list of the facts and phrases that are left and let them play with strategic line breaks to see how their poems might sound the best. The use of punctuation is optional.

I was fortunate one semester to have Maria as a student in my language arts methods course at the university. She loved writing poetry and songs. She worked in a group home for teenage girls. In fact, she stayed overnight in the home several nights a week. She chose to write her multigenre paper about these young women. Here is one poem she wrote that exemplifies a movement from stream of consciousness to verse:

In the Beginning

In the beginning
they come to us
they have nowhere else
they have no one else
they have been defeated and think the fight has just begun
they come to us wearing suits of armor and boxing gloves
they have no idea that we don't fight against them, but for
    them
they all have names, but have become numbers
they all have history that has been bound like a text book
they all have secrets that anyone can access
they all missed out on childhood because someone forced
    them to grow too fast
they all know too much but we cannot take their knowledge
    away
they all have nightmares which have been real
they all have dreams which have not been cultivated
they all have become children of the state
because no one else wanted them
and then they became ours
we become guards of their hard selves
they come to us grown
we try to give them back childhood
and raise them right
we try to give them the gift of a second chance

When Maria read her poem to our class, she not only helped us understand that poetry does not have to rhyme, but she also helped us understand the incredible odds some children have to face. The poem brought up serious issues and also led to a class discussion about the impact of her writing. Maria sifts through the layers of her life with these girls. She reveals her keen sense of who these young women are and how passionate she is to help them overcome insurmountable odds.

Double Voice

Tom Romano introduced me to double voice in *Writing with Passion* (1995). It is a writing technique used to express two sides of an issue within one piece of writing. He labels it a form of poetry. My students, the children, and I have written double voice poems often in our multigenre papers. Although this format can be used for lighthearted topics, it lends itself to more serious character self-reflection or an examination of conflicting opinions between people. Students find it easy to understand, yet quite powerful.

Brian, a fifth grader, wrote the following double voice poem in his multigenre paper about the Battle of Khe Sanh in the Vietnam War. He wrote from the perspective of a young soldier and his internal struggle with his commitment to the war.

Saying	Thinking
I can't wait to serve my country in Vietnam.	I hope I don't get killed, I'm scared.
I want to go and fight in Vietnam.	I would rather be a protestor at a college.
All of my friends will think I'm the coolest.	When I get home, my friends will hate me because I went to Vietnam.
What a chicken I would be if I didn't fight.	Maybe just getting arrested is better than going to Vietnam.
What should I do?	Go, fight.

The following is a double voice written by Jane, one of my university students. When Jane was in the eighth grade, her mother worked in a nursing home that had many elderly Jewish patients who were survivors of concentration camps. One day, Jane's mother invited one of the survivors to come speak to Jane's eighth-grade class. This incident, which she writes about in this double voice, made a lasting impression on Jane. When Jane read about double voice in Tom's book, it struck her as the perfect way to open her paper on the Holocaust. The thoughts on the left are those of the survivor; Jane's sentiments are expressed on the right.

Conflict

Look at them all laughing and talking
They don't know what pain is

                                        That poor man
                                        I wonder what he is thinking

How naïve
Stupid
Do they really want to know?

Time to start
What will he say?

Look at them
They stare at me
They don't believe

He's looking at me
What should I do?
Nod my head?

Blue eyes
Blonde hair
The Devil!!

Please
Look away
Stop it

You killed my brothers
My family
My people

Stop it!
Oh what the hell does he want
    from me!
Stop it!

Bitch!
Whore!
Murderer!

I didn't!
I didn't do it!
I'm on your side!

Poetry with Repetition and Rhythm

Another technique that can help students avoid rhyming schemes and
explore free verse is the use of repetition within a poem. Repetitive lines
can be inserted at strategic places in poems, can begin or end stanzas, or
can be used to signal breaks in continuity of form. Paula, who wrote her
multigenre research paper on her idol, Martin Luther King Jr., used a
repetitive questioning format to structure her poem. She also answered her
questions with a refrain that echoed her title. This repetition added rhythm.
When she read this poem during her oral presentation, it sounded like a
minister delivering a sermon, much like what King himself would do.

Who held you close when no one wanted to touch your
    darkened skin?
Who held you close when you were told the race wasn't yours
    to win?
Who held you close when you were almost beaten to death?

He did.
He did.

Who talked to you when you were told to shut the hell up?
Who talked to you when you were kicked in the mouth for
    praying for the freedom that you were born to deserve?
Who talked to you when you broke down and almost killed
    yourself before they had the satisfaction of killing you first?

He did.
He did.

Who promised to love you black, brown, white or purple?
Who promised to love you no matter what you'd go through?
Who promised to love you and stand by you forever?

He did.
He did.

Who stayed with you when they killed your mother . . . just
    because?
Who stayed with you when they threw you down and burned
    your skin . . . just because?
Who stayed with you when they said they would kill him if he
    didn't turn his back on you?

He did.
He did.

Who brought you to the Promise Land?
Who brought you to the top of the mountain?
Who brought you to the freedom?

He did.
He did.

The poetry mini-lessons in this chapter are simple ways to get students involved in a genre that can be very rewarding. There is a lot of flexibility in poetry writing and students who sometimes have difficulty writing long, connected text can be successful in this area. Without fail, every multigenre paper our students have written to date has contained one or more poems. Acrostic, list, and shape poems are easy to write yet can give the reader snippets of information in eye-catching arrangements. The double voice format has provided a good forum for the expression of internal conflict or multiple perspectives. Finally, the use of six-room poems, stream of conscious, and repetition have successfully introduced students to free verse. Multigenre papers would not seem complete if they didn't contain some poetic experiments.

In the next chapter we move on to character sketches. Since so many children choose people as the topics of their multigenre papers, spending some time getting to know a bit about characters gives them some ideas for their papers.

5

WHAT A CHARACTER
Bringing Subjects to Life

Some people just stand out in your mind. It's the way they move, or how they talk, or their wit that makes you say, "What a character!" I just loved Frank McCourt as a young boy in *Angela's Ashes*. He brought humor to such an incredibly impoverished existence. Good characters are central to good writing. They are also central to our multigenre research reports.

To be able to write successfully about a person, a student must know a lot about the person, she must get inside that person's skin, and she must write about that person from multiple perspectives. She must capture the essence of that person. She must learn to show, not tell.

Show, Don't Tell

I begin the discussion of characters by reading aloud excerpts from good writers. I start with a short story from Bailey White's book *Mama Makes Up Her Mind* (1995). In it, Bailey includes many humorous short stories about her Mama. A particular favorite of mine is called "Finger." In this story, Bailey talks about her Uncle Jimbuddy, a cabinetmaker who had been cutting off pieces of his fingers for ten years. One day Uncle Jimbuddy called Bailey and her Mama because he had a bushel of oysters to give them. When Mama and Bailey got to his shop, Jimbuddy's son, Ambrose, greeted them with cries that his dad had cut off his finger. He had only ten minutes to find it and get his dad to the hospital so they could sew it back on. Ambrose searched, but because Uncle Jimbuddy's shop was such a disastrous mess, he was forced to drive his father to the hospital without the finger. When Bailey and her Mama got into their car to head for home, her Mama asked Bailey to get out of the car and get the sack of oysters.

> "How can you think about oysters at a time like this?" Bailey asked. "I can always think about oysters," her Mama said. "Besides, Jimbuddy wouldn't want us to mope around drooling and starving and let those oysters rot in their sack just because he cut his finger off." (97)

When they got home, Mama went right to work at the sink opening and eating the oysters. After about ten oysters she found the finger and said,

"Why it's your Uncle Jimbuddy's finger!" And it was. Drained pale, shriveled, and ice cold, it didn't look like any part of a man I loved. Mama examined it dispassionately. "Well, he'll never have to worry about this hangnail again," she said. (97–98)

Bailey called her uncle to tell him Mama found his finger and to see how he was doing. Uncle Jimbuddy didn't seem upset but wanted to know what Mama did with his finger.

"What do you want her to do with it?" I asked Jimbuddy.
"I don't care what she does with it," he said. Then he added, as a cautionary afterthought, "Just don't let her eat it." (98)

I use this story because it is humorous and it provokes emotional comments from students. It really gets them involved. Students respond in a variety of ways:

"Oh, gross! That's terrible. Yuck."
"I loved it. I thought it was funny."
"I liked the finger. It's all shriveled and has a hangnail. I can really picture it."
"I liked Mama because she's like this really old ornery woman but not like regular old women because she doesn't mind eating oysters from a barrel with a finger floating around in it."
"I thought Uncle Jimbuddy was even more weird because he didn't mind losing the finger."

We talk about how Bailey uses detail and how she reveals her characters through their actions and dialogue. She doesn't tell us what they were like; she lets us discover them on our own.

I follow this discussion about Bailey's mother by reading the following excerpt from Ralph Fletcher's book *What a Writer Needs* (1993).

The boy rode on his brand new bicycle, down the driveway, onto the sidewalk and crash! He fell forward, right onto his face. He lay there motionless. The bike continued a few feet further before it, too, slammed into the pavement, the front wheel still spinning. With a cry his mother rushed down the driveway, past her son, and bent to examine the bicycle. (59)

This paragraph shows students a very different mother from Bailey's Mama. I ask them to tell me their thoughts. One student said to me, "God, she's a loser. All she cares about is the bike. She doesn't care about her son."

"Where does it say she doesn't care?" I asked.

"Well it doesn't, but look how she blew by the kid who was just on the ground motionless," the student replied.

We discuss how Ralph Fletcher, like Bailey White, shows us this mother through description without telling us about her. Fletcher says, "Put forth the raw evidence, and trust that the reader will understand exactly what you are getting at" (1993, 59). Showing, not telling, is the core of good character development, and it's hard to do.

To get students to develop the habit of showing instead of telling, we begin by carefully looking at people we want to write about. We have to slow down and look for detail and not thrust our thoughts and conclusions into the writing. One action I borrowed from Don Graves' book *Bring Life into Learning* (1999) is particularly helpful.

> ACTION: Take ten minutes to do a quick written sketch of a person you do not know. (10)

Children can observe someone in the lunchroom, outside before school, or in the community on weekends. One year, Christa wrote the following paragraph from an observation she made at a Dunkin' Donuts on a Saturday morning. I placed Christa's paragraph on an overhead and asked the children to tell me what pieces of the paragraph tell rather than show. Showing describes the scene as something is taking place with plenty of description, telling lets the writer sneak into the text with interpretations and conclusions. I underlined the parts we decided were telling.

> He sat with his head resting on his hand while reading the newspaper. He did not shave and was wearing a green and blue flannel shirt with a pair of blue jeans and work boots. He had short brown hair parted to the left and brown eyes. He wasn't a very big man. He was right handed and drank his coffee with his left hand. He would lift his head, take a bite of his bagel, wipe his face and proceed reading. He seemed to be in his own little world, not paying attention to anyone walking around or others having a conversation nearby. He was careful to turn the pages and make sure the paper stayed neat. When he was done reading he folded the paper, picked up his mess, and wiped down the table. He then threw his mess away and placed the newspaper on another table for someone else to read and walked toward the door. He was very relaxed and didn't seem to be in any kind of a rush.

When we finished, I asked the children to help me change the underlined parts so that the paragraph would show, not tell, us about the man in Dunkin' Donuts. One student suggested, "Instead of saying he wasn't very big, 'cause then we really don't know how big he is, maybe she could say he was about five feet three inches tall."

"Christa, how did you know he was right-handed?" I asked.

She replied, "He was basically eating the whole time with his right hand but would grab the coffee cup with his left. I don't know if that's important to even include. Maybe not."

"How could Christa show that he's in his own little world?" I asked.

"She could say just the rest of the sentence, and we'd know he was in his own world 'cause if he's not paying attention, he's just reading. You know how you can get lost in a book," one child offered.

"How does she know that he is leaving the paper for someone else to read?" I asked.

"That's what people do when they're finished with papers sometimes, but maybe he just didn't want to be bothered carrying the paper away with him," replied a student.

Another chimed in, "Yeah, but that doesn't make sense because if he was neat and clean about his mess, he would have thrown the paper away, too. He doesn't seem like a litterbug."

"When she doesn't say, we really don't know why, and that leaves it up to the reader. You want to do that in your writing. At the very end she says that he's very relaxed and not in a rush. How could she show him relaxed rather than tell us he is relaxed? Christa, what made you think he was relaxed?" I continued.

"It just seemed that he took a long time to get to the door and then he left and walked down the sidewalk slowly," she explained.

"Maybe we could say he drifted toward the door and then sauntered down the sidewalk," I suggested.

After students have the chance to hear excerpts from good writers like Bailey White and Ralph Fletcher, and then write and discuss quick sketches of people they don't know, we move ahead to create a character together.

Create a Class Character
Several years back when I was first trying to find an exercise that would help my students with character development, Don Graves sent me a list of questions that his friend Don Murray uses to brainstorm ideas for characters. I modified and reduced the list, and you will probably want to do the same. I've tried this exercise with both university and elementary students.

I ask each of my students to take out a piece of paper and number it from one to thirty-four. I read a list of questions and students take turns calling out answers. We sometimes argue about an answer, but we make a group decision and then write the answer on our papers. When we have completed the list, I distribute a photocopy of the questions. If I give them the list beforehand, they busy themselves reading the questions rather than paying attention to one another's responses. Below is the list with one class' responses.

1. What is your character's name?
   Gertrude McDowel

2. How old is your character?
   72

3. What does he or she look like?
   She has silver hair with a purple tinge. She always wears dark glasses.

4. How does he or she dress?
   She wears a long trench coat, a hat with plumes, and pink fuzzy slippers.

5. How does your character feel about his or her face and body?
   She flaunts her body and feels most proud about her belly button.

6. How is his or her voice? And does he or she have an accent?
   She has a husky voice.

7. What does he or she do when he or she gets angry?
   She shakes and spits.

8. What does he or she do when he or she gets depressed?
   She ignores everyone.

9. Where and how was he or she educated?
   She was educated in the South and graduated from high school.

10. What is his or her occupation?
    She was a dance hall queen.

11. Is that what the parents expected him or her to do?
    Her parents didn't expect anything. She ran away right after high school.

12. At what age did your character first work? What was the job?
    She worked at 18 as a cocktail waitress.

13. What was the best or worst job your character had?
    At one time she was a baker.

14. Where was your character born?
    She was born in Mobile, Alabama.

15. Does your character have any siblings?
    Yes, she has one brother.

16. Does your character have any other important relatives?
    Yes, a daughter.

17. What kind of vehicle does your character drive?
    She drives a station wagon.

18. Where does your character live? How does he or she feel about the place?
    She lives in New York City and likes it.

19. Is your character married or living with someone?
    She is a widow.

20. If your character has children, do they live with him or her?
    Her daughter does not live with her.

21. What is your character's relationship with his or her parents and siblings?
    Her parents are no longer alive. She had a good relationship with her brother.
22. What was your character's first experience with death in or out of the family?
    Her brother died in the Vietnam War.
23. Who is your character's best friend?
    Her dog.
24. If your character were to confide in someone, who would it be?
    Her daughter.
25. If your character could have any wish, what would it be?
    She wants true love.
26. What does your character do for fun?
    She goes to the park and to the beach.
27. What is your character's favorite food?
    Pinto beans and lemon pie.
28. Set your character in motion across a room and describe how he or she moves.
    She struts.
29. Does your character have any pets?
    Yes, a dog.
30. What is your character's biggest fear?
    She is afraid she is going to die alone.
31. What is your character's religious affiliation, if any?
    She is a Baptist.
32. What does your character really believe in?
    Reincarnation.
33. Does your character have a nickname?
    Trixie.
34. How often does your character fall in love and what does he or she do about it?
    She has never been in love.

The pace is fast and furious. As quickly as I read the questions, my students call out the answers. At times we get laughing so hard I lose my place. One response sparks the next. I have done this exercise with many classes, and the characters each class produces are all so different. When we've finished the list, I send them off with a task: "As part of your assignment this week you have to write a short piece of fiction incorporating some of the information about Trixie. Remember that this list helps us understand what our character is like. You are not to use all this information in your story.

Create a scene where you *show* us Trixie in action. Don't *tell* us about her. Try to grasp the essence of Trixie."

I give them several days to complete the task. At our next meeting I ask for volunteers to read their pieces. With a little coaxing, Amy read hers.

> Gertrude was standing in the middle of Grand Central Station.
>
> "She'll be comin' 'round the mountain when she come," she sang softly in her deep, husky voice.
>
> The next verse she sang a little bit louder. "She'll be comin' 'round that mountain when she come!"
>
> Suddenly Gertrude sang the rest of the words at the top of her lungs, "She'll be comin' 'round the mountain, she be around that mountain when she cooome!!"
>
> "Trixie!!!" called the police officer guarding the station. "Quiet down over there!!"
>
> Gertrude slowly started towards the officer, strutting and unfastening her buttons. She then began to shake her shoulders back and forth, and turned her head to the right and spit on the ground. When she was standing five feet in front of the officer, she flashed open her trench coat exposing her stained pink bra and matching bloomers she had bought at the Salvation Army for $3.50 the year before.
>
> "Enough of that, Trixie!! You don't want me to have to take you in again, do ya?" asked the frustrated officer, as he had arrested Trixie ten too many times for disorderly conduct.
>
> "You just go 'bout that bi'ness you got yerself into, copper!" she snuffed. Her body began to shake violently. She turned her head to the left and again spit onto the floor. She then clapped her hands several times and her body stopped shaking. She closed her coat and stomped her foot while snarling at the officer.
>
> "I is waitin' for my kinfolk, Mister, and you ain't gonna tell me otherwise, ya hear me copper?"
>
> The police officer began to feel a little sympathetic for old Trixie and replied, "Okay. You go on and wait. Just pipe down while you're waiting, huh?" He put his right hand on his gun holster, turned, and walked away whistling, "She'll be coming 'round the mountain."
>
> "Dang nabbit copper!! He don't know nothin' bout my baby! She be comin' to see me soon, I just know it."
>
> Gertrude folded her wrinkled hands behind her back and began strutting to and fro. She headed for the outside door dragging her feet along the floor so as not to kick off her pink bunny slippers. She opened the door quickly, put on her dark glasses

and walked to the other side of the sidewalk where she had tied her dog to the newspaper rack.

"Hi-a pooch!"

The yellow lab, whose fur was dirty and stuck together in clumps in some places, began to wag his tail excitedly. He gave a bark in Trixie's direction.

"How's about a lickin' for good old Trixie? That a good pooch!" She carefully untied his leash from the rack and wrapped the end around her small wrist. The two scruffy images walked down the city sidewalk.

"Let's find some beans and pie, poochie. She be comin' 'round the mountain soon. I just know it."

When Amy finished reading her piece we talked about it.

"Do you think that Amy captured the essence of Trixie?" I asked.

"Yes, I totally loved the way she wrote about Trixie," one student replied.

"What details did she incorporate? Check your lists." I said.

A student offered, "Let's see, she used both her name and nickname and the fact that she came from the South. You could tell that from her husky Southern accent."

"Also she wears dark glasses, a trench coat, and those pink slippers," another added.

"Grand Central Station is in New York so we know she's there, and also she gets the dog in by tying him up outside. You know Trixie likes him because she wants a kiss from him and she wants to get dinner for the both of them," a third supplied.

"What is Trixie like?" I asked.

"She seems lonely because she's waiting for her daughter, who isn't coming. She must go to the station a lot because she's been picked up by the police before," a student replied.

Another student said, "She doesn't have money and seems almost to be a street person. I feel bad for her."

Amy used detail and dialogue and showed us Trixie without telling us about her. Amy's piece of fiction is very different from those written by other members of the class. Each student had his or her own version of Trixie. We shared some of the other scenarios. When we finished our character exercises, students placed their lists of questions and their character sketches in their notebooks for future reference.

Our create-a-character exercise translates well into our multigenre projects. Our students become the resident experts on their topics. They can generate their own long lists of information about characters or events. From that list, some will choose to write fictional pieces similar to Amy's experiment with Trixie.

Model a Quickwrite, Then Revise

Sometimes at the beginning of the multigenre project, children can't get going. The writing seems overwhelming. For some, the project seems like the hardest thing they will ever have to do. We have to assure them that writing, is difficult at first, even for the best of writers. It is a process that takes time. We can teach our students this through modeling.

I begin at home by watching a two-minute segment of a video. I stop the video and write a summary of it without looking back. When I write this quickly, I don't have time to think about my writing. I write to get the information down and my draft needs lots of help. I wrote the following paragraph after watching a few-minute segment from the video *Andrea Bocelli: A Night in Tuscany* (1997). I typed and distributed my first draft to my students. They had not seen the video. I read it aloud as they read it silently.

Draft 1

Andrea and Enrica walk along the beach. Andrea carries Amos on his shoulders. You can hear the sound of the waves in the background. They are smiling and chatting. Later Amos gets two sticks and walks along in the sand by himself.

Later Andrea and Amos sit quietly on a chair and talk. Amos listens to his father and the lays his head against his father's chest. They seem to enjoy each other's company.

First I asked my students two questions:

1. What didn't you understand about the draft?
2. What do you want to know more about?

Here are their comments:

1. What do they look like?
2. How old is Amos?
3. What beach was it?
4. Was it day or night? Sunrise or sunset?
5. Were there other people around?
6. The pronouns are not clear.
7. Why are they there?
8. It lacks description.
9. What was the weather like?
10. Were the waves crashing?

I wrote their responses on the board so they could copy them into their notebooks. I based my first revision on these responses. The first time I model revision, I do my writing at home because I like to give my students typed copies of all the drafts of my writing.

Here is the result of my first revision. I distributed this to the class and read it aloud.

Draft 2

Andrea and Enrica walk along the beach on the Italian Rivera. Andrea carries their three-year-old son Amos on his shoulders. It is about 85 degrees and the sky is bright blue. Blue and red beach chairs are lined up from the lime green beach houses to the water. Many mothers and children are digging in the sand. Andrea wears a dark T-shirt and baggie shorts. His dark brown hair is blowing in the warm ocean breeze. Waves are gently lapping the shoreline. Enrica's brown hair is pulled back in a bun and her printed dress wraps around her legs. Occasionally she smiles broadly and her white teeth flash in the sunshine. Little Amos is bare footed and wears a striped sleeveless shirt and a bathing suit. Andrea lowers Amos down and he runs along the edge of the water. The parents are smiling and chatting as they follow Amos down the beach. He picks up two waterlogged sticks, one for each hand, and walks along in the hot sand by himself. He is swinging the sticks in the air, pointing to something out in the sea, and talking to himself.

Later Amos sits on Andrea's lap on a beach chair in the shade. A thatched roof of straw protects them from the blazing noon sun. They are talking about what fun it is to be at the beach. Amos looks up at his father and then lays his head against his father's chest. They seem to enjoy each other's company.

My students and I discussed how I answered some of their questions and how I added detail. While they had this draft in front of them I talked to them about the most powerful aspect in all writing, the verb. Verbs are the engines of sentences. They should be strong and precise. Weak verbs are those that use the helping verbs *is* and *are*, like *is blowing* and *are lapping,* and those verbs that end with prepositions, like *works on* and *closes up.* Precise verbs are descriptive and carry the meaning of the sentence. Drab verbs such as *walks, talks,* and *saw* should be replaced with verbs like *strolled, gossiped,* and *glanced.*

My students and I circled all the verbs in my piece. Our goal was to strengthen them. We went to work and changed the verbs to *dig, lap, smile, chat, swings, points, talks,* and *talk.* We replaced the verbs that were followed by prepositions and we brainstormed more exciting verbs to eliminate drab ones like *walk.* I took their suggestions home to revise and retype my piece. I brought them a clean copy and we proceeded to the next step in our revision process—eliminating extras.

Kill Clichés. I read my students some of the following examples. Once they understand what a cliché is, they brainstorm some of their own. Here is a list your students can place in their notebooks for future reference. Also have them add to the list.

avoid like the plague
dead serious
heart to heart
water under the bridge
bone to pick
head and shoulders above the rest
take with a grain of salt
hill of beans
dull as dishwater
happy as a clam
hit the nail on the head
worn to a frazzle
on the tip of your tongue
cute as a button
uphill battle
a tough row to hoe
stubborn as a mule
stick in the mud
bend your ear
put your nose to the grindstone
don't look a gift horse in the mouth
bright as a button
plain as the nose on your face
don't count your chickens before they hatch
don't beat around the bush
keep a stiff upper lip
all in the eye of the beholder
in a nutshell

As it happened, I didn't have any clichés in my piece about the beach, but clichés like these inevitably show up in students' writing and can be the first and easiest items to eliminate.

Remove fillers. Delete fillers like *sort of, kind of, occasionally, it seems,* and *it appears.* This is wishy-washy writing, as in the last sentence of my revised piece, when I wrote, "They seem to enjoy each other's company." They either *do* or they *don't.* Ask the writer to make the decision.

Avoid repeating the same word. I made this mistake at the beginning of the piece when I used the word *blue* to describe the sky and the beach chairs. I had to eliminate one of them.

Keep sentences and paragraphs concise.   When sentences and paragraphs get too long, you lose the reader. We crossed out several sentences or parts of sentences that we felt were unnecessary. We also discussed ways to divide the first long paragraph into several shorter ones.

Read your draft aloud.   When you think you have completed all revisions, read the piece aloud. When I did this, a student brought up an important point: "You know what's missing? You write that Amos and his father are talking about what fun they are having at the beach. Let them say it. Remember the dialogue in Bailey White's story about Mama and Amy's story about Trixie?" Right. How could I forget that? I went home, made my final revisions, and typed copies for my students. Here is the final draft.

At Peace with the Sea

Andrea and Enrica stroll along the beach on the Italian Rivera. Andrea carries their three-year-old son Amos on his shoulders. The sapphire blue sky sets the perfect backdrop for the red canvas beach chairs lined up from the bath houses to the water.

Andrea wears a black T-shirt and baggy shorts. His dark brown hair blows in the warm ocean breeze. To help her stay cool, Enrica has tied her silky, brown hair in a bun. Her beach dress, rich with earthtones, wraps around her legs. Andrea lowers Amos to the ground and the boy races to the water. Enrica watches Amos splash his feet in the waves that lap the shoreline. She smiles broadly and her white teeth flash in the sunshine.

Little Amos wears a bathing suit and a blue and white striped shirt to protect him from the sun. He retrieves two waterlogged sticks from the sea, one for each hand. He dots the shore with footprints as he swings the sticks in the air. He points to something out at sea and talks to himself.

Enrica leaves Amos and Andrea in the shade by a beach house. Amos sits on Andrea's lap on a beach chair. A thatched roof of straw protects them from the blazing noon sun.

"Papa," says Amos, "I love to come to the beach and I'm so glad that you are with me and Mamma today."

"I'm happy too. When I come home from my tours there is nothing I love more than to be with you and your mother."

Amos stares at his father for several seconds and then lays his head against his father's chest. The two sit silently together and listen to the sounds of the sea.

After reading the final draft to my students, I played the segment of the video that inspired it. It was fun to see if what I wrote compared to what they saw through their own eyes.

Here is a copy of a quick checklist to remind students of the steps they can take to improve their writing.

- Read lots of pieces of writing with good characters.
- Practice writing character sketches in which you show, don't tell.
- Write quick drafts, changing nothing the first time through.
- Follow these revision steps:
    Add details.
    Strengthen verbs.
    Eliminate extras.
    Shorten sentences and paragraphs.
    Add dialogue.

Depending upon how much time you have designated for the multigenre project, you might want to try the show, don't tell and create-a-character exercises mentioned at the beginning of this chapter before your students begin their research. You can save the quickwrites and revision exercises for the time when your students are writing pieces for their multigenre papers. You might want them to spend time revising actual pieces for their papers.

In this chapter and the last, I've taken a look at poetic surprises and had some fun with characters and revision. Now it's time to look at nonfiction, which constitutes most of what we write in our everyday lives. Children also write the majority of their pieces for their multigenre papers in nonfiction. The nonfiction samples suggested in the next chapter will complete your students' introduction to genres. Then they can begin their research.

THE VOICE OF NONFICTION
Valuing Real, Everyday Writing

6

> When we write about something we care about, something in which we have an emotional stake, our writing automatically acquires "voice." (Cameron 1998, 160)

After working with students on multigenre projects for the past four years, I've learned that students express their emotions best through nonfiction. Some rely on nonfiction because it is what they are most used to reading in their daily encounters; others use nonfiction because it provides such a variety of ways for self-expression. Whatever the reason, nonfiction makes students' voices heard.

Nonfiction also gives students the opportunity to write from a number of points of view. As you will see in the student writing samples that follow in this chapter, students readily take the first-person point of view of children, newscasters, book reviewers, and newspaper writers. Throughout their papers they can easily step from their more egocentric selves into a variety of personas to explain their research. Once a student becomes the resident expert on his topic, he speaks not only from the point of view of the person he is researching but also from the point of view of any number of people involved in his main character's life. This chance to inhabit different points of view helps students think differently. Unlike the traditional research paper, in which the author writes from the impersonal third person, multigenre pieces encourage and inspire students to learn and express themselves differently. Multigenre pieces make the research come alive.

Each year I write a multigenre research paper along with my students. It is very important for them to see me attempting to tackle a subject. I share with them how I read and jot notes in the margins to remind myself of important facts. I keep my list of genres nearby (see list on p. 71) so I can brainstorm combinations between facts and genres. I try a number of nonfiction genres and share them. These drafts of my writing show students that teachers are not perfect. Truly consider doing a multigenre paper with your students the first time you have them do one. You will bring credibility to the whole project.

One year I wrote my multigenre research paper on Italian immigration. I thought that the reader should have a brief, factual introduction, or an advanced organizer, so that the rest of the pieces in my paper would make sense. So for my first piece I wrote the following short encyclopedia entry to accomplish this goal.

> ITALIAN IMMIGRATION. Italian immigrants or emigrants might better be labeled migrant workers because that was the primary purpose why most of the Italians left their homeland. Most Northern Italians went to Brazil or Argentina while most Southern Italians went to the United States. Between the years of 1820 and 1963, five million Italians immigrated to the U.S. These immigrants comprised about 30% of all Italians who left their country. The primary ports of embarkation were Naples, Palermo, and Genoa. Most immigrants were between the ages of 25 and 40 and the males outnumbered the females three to one. About 65% of the immigrants were cultivators, tenant farmers, field workers and shepherds. Approximately 20% were masons, carpenters, stonecutters, bakers, blacksmiths, cooks, shoemakers, barbers, tailors, and miners. The remaining immigrants were doctors, lawyers, teachers, accountants, pharmacists, and housewives.
>
> In 1910, Italians, along with other immigrants from Southern and Eastern Europe, made up one half of America's labor force. They primarily worked in Chicago slaughterhouses, New England textile mills, Pennsylvania coal mines, and New York clothing factories. One third of all Italian immigrants settled in New York and the rest located primarily in Massachusetts, Rhode Island, and California.

Laurie believes that it is important for her children to be able to write expository text. She also feels that it is important for them to provide background information in their papers. So, just like I wrote a brief encyclopedia opening to my paper on immigration, we have the children write a minimum two-page expository piece in which they must summarize concisely the results of their research. Children often find this the most difficult piece to write because they must analyze and synthesize all their material. Once they have done this, however, the remaining pieces in their papers grow naturally from it.

Each year students want to know how many pieces they have to include in their papers. We work this out together, and I will describe that process later on, but in addition to the two- to four-page research piece, Laurie most recently required three poems and a minimum of ten pieces. To help our students build a repertoire of genres, Laurie and I give our students the following list of more than one hundred nonfiction ideas. Each year the list grows as students write additional genres to meet the needs of their papers.

They place this list in their Resource Notebooks. The genres that appear in this chapter are marked with asterisks. Those genres marked with plus signs are the ones that have most often been selected by students to include in their papers.

Genres

*+ ads	epitaphs	parodies
allegories	* encyclopedia entries	plays
+ announcements	essays	+ poems
autobiographies	+ eulogies	+ posters
+ awards	fables	+ postcards
baseball cards	+ family trees	* prayers
bedtime stories	flip books	propaganda sheets
billboards	game rules	product descriptions
biographies	graffiti	puppet shows
book jackets	good news/bad news	+ puzzles
* book reviews	*+ grocery lists	+ questionnaires
+ brochures	+ headlines	+ questions
+ bulletins	how-to speeches	+ quizzes
*+ bumper stickers	impromptu speeches	+ quotations
calendars	*+ interviews	real estate notices
campaign speeches	job applications	*+ recipes
+ captions	+ journals	remedies
+ cartoons	laboratory notes	requests
+ certificates	*+ letters	requisitions
character sketches	+ lists	+ research pieces
children's books	lyrics	*+ resumés
comic strips	magazines	reviews
contracts	maps	riddles
conversations	memos	sales pitches
critiques	memoirs	schedules
+ crossword puzzles	*+ menus	slogans
course syllabi	mission statements	+ speeches
* dedications	mysteries	stamps
+ definitions	myths	stickers
*+ diaries	*+ newscasts	+ tables of contents
* diplomas	newsletters	TV commercials
*+ directions	*+ newspapers	+ telegrams
directories	*+ obituaries	*+ tickets
+ double voice poems	observational notes	+ time lines
editorials	+ pamphlets	* tombstones
		tributes
		Web pages
		+ webs
		*+ word searches
		*+ wills

Student Writing Samples

The best way for students to grasp the concept of multigenre research papers is to look at papers written by former students, both elementary and university. But prior to the sharing of full-length papers I share different samples from selected papers to help students see how former students utilized different genres to meet the needs of their topics. This also gives students an introduction to some of the topics former students have chosen.

Dayna wrote her paper on David Helfgott, the pianist who was the subject of the movie *Shine*. He lived quite a tormented life because his father did not want him to leave the family to study music. David went away in spite of his father's wishes and spent the rest of his days trying to win his father's favor. Dayna had seen the movie and was intrigued. She really wanted to know more about him. Amidst a paper dotted with photos, poetry, famous quotes, and newspaper articles was the following concert ticket.

Aisle: 2 Row G Seat:5	***The Wang Centre*** ***For The Performing Arts*** David Helfgott Live September 19, 1996 7:30 PM	*Aisle: 2* Row: G Seat: 5
Ticket invalid Without this Portion	 Non Refundable	This portion to be taken by Theatre

FIGURE 6–1.   Concert ticket

With this small ticket, Dayna was able to show us that David became famous enough to perform at the prestigious Wang Centre in Massachusetts. She didn't tell us how famous he was but let us draw our own conclusions.

Willa wrote her multigenre paper on Lewis Carroll. She absolutely loved *Alice in Wonderland* and would often quote from it. During her research she found that Carroll, in addition to being an author, liked photography. Willa experimented with block printing and carved the outline of one of Carroll's cameras into a wood block. Willa wanted to express herself artistically but also felt the need to explain how she tackled this new project. As one of her genres she wrote this how-to list of directions.

How I Made My Wood Block Print

I took a piece of linoleum (not the kind you put on floors)
I carved an old fashioned camera into it
I covered the side I had drawn a camera on with white paint
I laid a piece of black paper on the print and pressed down on it

I removed the paper and let it dry
The camera illustrated on the black paper is the kind Charles Dodgson
(Lewis Carroll) used

The Oklahoma City bombing had taken place a year before Charisa became a student in my language arts class. She decided to write about it in her paper because one of her friends lived in Oklahoma City, and her friend's husband was one of the firefighters who participated in the rescue. Charisa imagined how a two-year-old might write his will. In this piece, Charisa mixed fact and fiction, which is common in multigenre research papers. Although a two-year-old could not possibly write or understand the concept of a will, from this point of view, Charisa was able to capture the tragedy of the bombing.

> I, Colton Wade Smith, age two, leave my favorite pacifier with the teddies on it to my brand new baby brother, Chase. I wish my best friend Joshua from my playgroup to have my favorite ball, the big, red, bouncy one. I would like my friend Christopher, who lived down the street from me and my mommy to have my sandbox. We always played together in the sand at my house. I would like my other friend Nicholas to have my new, shiny tricycle that my daddy got me for my birthday. Finally, I wish my mommy to have my Barney and my snuggly blanket that I used to sleep with so that when she gets sad, it will make her feel better.
>
> Love,
> Colton

Another piece Charisa included in her paper was this news bulletin. Students are very familiar with this genre and hear it often on television and radio. It is a very effective way to introduce facts and begin a paper.

> We interrupt this program for a special news bulletin. There has been a major explosion in the Alfred P. Murrah Building in downtown Oklahoma City shortly after 9:00 A.M. Central/Standard time. Initial reports are sketchy. All that is known at this time is that there is severe structural damage to the building itself and the number of casualties is unknown. Stay tuned for more details. We will interrupt future programming to bring you updates live from the scene in Oklahoma City.

Children are used to receiving certificates for being student of the month, having perfect attendance, participating in a science fair, and a score of other achievements. Often they use this genre to reveal the outstanding accomplishments of the people they choose for their papers. Many use computer programs to make their certificates look very professional.

Many of us, no matter what age, keep diaries and journals. Serious writers carry small notebooks with them every day and record snippets that might be used in future pieces. I always keep a journal when I go on a trip to remind me of all the wonderful sights I have seen. Kyle wrote his paper on Babe Ruth. Babe's wife was killed in a fire and Kyle wrote this entry for the day of the tragedy.

January 11, 1929

Dear Diary,

A fire killed Helen this morning at 10:00 A.M. There was no way to save her because the walls collapsed on her and she smothered in the smoke.

Dorothy is a wreck, so I am sending her to boarding school so I can find a house for us. I also don't want her to be reminded by all of Helen's belongings that were retrieved from the fire.

After six years of marriage, I lose my first love to a stupid fire that was caused by a candle. I will visit her grave every day but it will only soothe my pain in the smallest amount. I myself am discouraged, but I can't show Dorothy that I am weak and still try to tell her to keep fighting the pain.

I'm not even sure if I will return to the field right away, but I'm leaning more towards going back to my career so I can support Dorothy.

I must go tell Dorothy that she is going to boarding school.

Sincerely,

George

Many students use diary entries in their papers. They often scatter them throughout the papers as a unifying element. The reader witnesses different events and then views them from the perspective of the person writing the diary. It gives students the chance to interject interpretations and emotions.

Sometimes a book a student has read might inspire her to choose a topic for her multigenre topic. Gina read *My Sergei,* written by the Russian skater Ekaterina Gordeeva about her husband and pairs partner, Sergei. Although in his twenties, he died of a heart attack while completing one of his routines. When Gina finished the book, she decided not only to write her paper about Sergei but also to write a book review as one of her genres.

My Sergei: A Love Story

By Ekaterina Gordeeva (with E. M. Swift)
Warner, November 1996, $18.95, hardcover, 292 pages,
ISBN 0-446-52087-X

If you are a true romantic, you must read the book Ekaterina Gordeeva, famous pairs figure skater from Russia, wrote as a tribute to her beloved partner and husband, Sergei Grinkov. Gordeeva tells the story of her life with Sergei, from being paired together as children to Grinkov's tragic and sudden death of a heart attack at the age of 28. He died on the ice in the arms of his wife. The 292-page book has two eight-page sections of color photos, as well as many black and white pictures spread throughout the book.

Another interesting aspect of the book is Katia's perspective on being an athlete under the old Soviet system. As her career with Sergei, with gold medals in the 1988 and 1994 Olympics, was on the upswing, the fate of the former Soviet Union was on the way down.

Once you start reading this book, it is almost impossible to stop. I read it during the course of one day, alternating between laughing and crying. Katia tells this amazing story from her heart, and in the process, she exposes her innermost feelings.

Katia and Sergei's story is a unique one. Not only were they Olympic Champions, but they fell in love, got married, became parents, and returned to the ice to win yet another gold medal in 1994, all while in the eye of the adoring public. It is one of the best true love stories ever told.

This book has been in the #1 or #2 spot on the best seller list since it was released a few weeks ago. As of now, it has sold over 700,000 copies, and I can honestly see why. Katia's courage and determination are an inspiration.

Again through this book review, we see a melding of fact and emotion. Gina wanted to share her passion for the book. When she shared this piece with others in the class, they too wanted to read the book.

During our first year of writing multigenre papers, Ryan White had recently died of AIDS. Controversy over his attendance in school and exposure to AIDS in general was of great concern. Amy wrote her paper about Ryan White. One of the pieces she included was the bumper sticker shown in Figure 6–2:

A.I.D.S
Spread the word
not the disease.

FIGURE 6–2.

Students like to include bumper stickers in their papers. The challenge for them is to express themselves in clever ways with a minimal number of words.

When Diana, princess of Wales, died in a terrible car crash, people around the world mourned her death. Her humanitarian deeds and her endearing personality left an indelible impression, especially upon Alyssa. In her paper, Alyssa took the viewpoint of Harry, one of Diana's sons, and wrote a letter to his mother.

Dear Mummy,

William told me that he was writing to you, and said he would help me do the same. I miss you so much. I do not understand why God has taken you away from us. Daddy told us that you are at peace now, helping God do His work. Doesn't God know that we need you? People have told me that you are with me all of the time, even though I cannot see you, and that makes me feel a little bit better. But I want to be able to see you again. I would give you the biggest hug ever. It would be so big that when I let go you would still feel my arms wrapped around you. I just wish I could have the chance to show you. Daddy told me that I could still talk to you, and even though you won't talk back you will be able to hear me. I will, Mummy, I will talk to you every night before I go to bed. Mummy, I love you.

Love,

Harry

Letters are a very popular genre among students. They find it easy to take the points of view of other young people with whom they can identify. These pieces usually contain strong voices.

Those of us who are old enough can remember Christa McAuliffe and the explosion of the Challenger. I remember exactly where I was standing when I first heard the news. As part of her multigenre paper on the Challenger, Alison decided to interview people to see if they could remember where they were when they first heard the news. Here is one of the responses.

Where Were You?????

I was sitting in the ninth grade English class, when the librarian came busting into the room screaming that the shuttle had exploded. At first I thought, "What shuttle is she talking about?" The girl sitting next to me said, "The Challenger? That's the one with the teacher on it, isn't it?" The whole school rushed down and packed into the library where we sat for the rest of the day watching the explosion over and over and over again.

B. E.

Alison included several quotes like this one. They brought humanity to her paper.

Children are also very familiar with word searches and crossword puzzles. These genres provide them with the opportunity to use many of the major vocabulary words they acquire during their investigations. Web sites like the following can help them input their information and display it in a very pleasing format: *http://www.Shareware.com* and *http://puzzlemaker. school.discovery.com*. Annalisa wrote a word search about Amelia Earhart.

WORD SEARCH

M	O	G	Q	N	F	R	C	P	U	P	S	O	R	G	D
Y	B	A	C	O	Y	I	P	Q	N	U	A	R	R	Y	S
T	F	P	T	O	T	A	O	A	H	S	A	R	C	K	R
H	W	O	S	N	H	S	M	T	U	V	L	C	L	Q	D
S	O	Q	A	A	G	E	H	I	E	O	F	G	O	D	E
G	B	L	B	N	G	O	F	T	S	U	O	Q	U	E	A
R	T	R	R	A	I	F	L	I	G	H	T	O	D	S	F
A	A	B	B	T	N	O	Y	O	N	O	S	N	S	R	B
G	B	R	I	D	D	C	C	D	Z	W	W	W	E	R	T
V	A	V	C	V	I	E	I	G	H	R	O	D	E	V	D
G	E	R	Q	U	A	A	T	C	H	I	S	O	N	D	O
G	C	B	X	Y	Z	N	O	R	L	Q	L	H	O	S	T
S	E	M	I	A	M	I	M	E	G	E	E	O	O	T	F
R	L	L	Q	J	T	R	O	R	R	B	D	N	N	U	R
W	X	E	O	M	A	I	L	E	M	A	D	I	A	N	A
S	O	Q	I	R	M	O	D	D	H	M	B	T	N	T	R
S	H	R	T	G	U	X	S	S	Y	Z	R	Q	U	F	T
B	C	A	L	D	H	F	E	E	K	A	N	S	A	S	E
O	Q	O	H	D	O	R	O	A	O	B	O	C	O	M	E

AMELIA	FRED	OCEAN
ATCHISON	GARBAGE MAN	RED SEA
ATLANTIC	INDIA	SLED
CLOUDS	KANSAS	SLEIGH
CRASH	MIAMI	STUNT
DEAF	MYTHS	UP
FLIGHT	NOONAN	WORLD
FLY		

FIGURE 6–3.

Chris was taking trumpet lessons and was interested in knowing more about Louis Armstrong. It is good for students to write multigenre papers about people who have professions or hobbies with which they can identify. It helps them learn more about themselves and about the professions they might like to pursue in the future. Here is one of Chris' pieces about Louis.

Obituary

July 7, 1971

Louis Armstrong 1901–1971

Louis Armstrong, 70, of New Orleans, died yesterday, July 6, 1971, in his home in New Orleans. He died of old age.

Born in New Orleans on August 4, 1901, he was the son of Mayann Armstrong. He started playing the trumpet at age 12. He apprenticed with his idol Joe "King" Oliver. He later joined Joe Oliver's band in 1922.

The world of Jazz was never the same after Louis Armstrong teamed up with Johnny St. Cry, Johnny Dodds, Kid Ory, and Lil Harden to form the "Hot Five." Armstrong was the band's featured performer and became world famous.

Armstrong was well liked by the people of the United States and the world. Many called him Ambassador of Good Will because he brought pleasure to all groups regardless of nationality, color, or creed. He loved human beings everywhere and sought to make everybody happy.

Special memorial services will be held for Armstrong all over the country. His funeral will be held next Friday in New Orleans. Three Jazz bands will be playing at the ceremony. The ceremony will have prayers and speeches from the Mayor and the local minister. In a few weeks a ceremony will be held in Chicago. Louis' wife, Lillian Harding Armstrong, will take part in the ceremony.

Students tend to use birth announcements, death certificates, obituaries, and eulogies to signal the beginnings and ends of their papers. They fit naturally into the chronology of the papers.

Leah, an art minor, was enthralled with Vincent van Gogh. During the time she was writing her paper, she even painted a copy of one of his paintings. Van Gogh was a tormented artist who led a tortured life. As a unique representation of his death, she drew a tombstone with the following engraving.

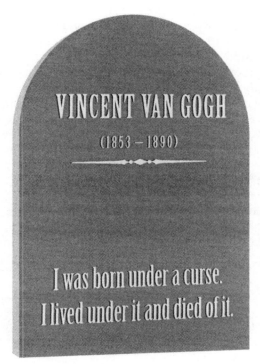

FIGURE 6–4. Tombstone

Kelly wrote her paper on a particular favorite of mine, Tina Turner. Using different computer fonts and downloading photos of Tina from the Internet, she created a newspaper article. The Internet and computer technology have really allowed students to become creative in the representation of their papers. I would encourage students to print several good photos when they get the chance to use the Internet. Here's what Kelly wrote.

Tina Turner Is Back

April 30, 1998

Solo and Stronger Than Ever

Roger Davies became Turner's manager in 1979 and began to turn things around for her. Turner began touring places such as South Africa, Australia, and the Far East. The tour was a success but Davies was growing less and less happy with Tina's show. He felt the show wasn't right for her and was missing something. Turner and Davies found new musicians and together they decided they needed to play rock and roll.

Tina made a two-week record in London. On it, Tina seemed to tell the story of her whole life in just nine songs from "Better Be Good to Me" to "I Might Have Been Queen." Tina showed that she could sing pop, rhythm and blues, reggae, heavy metal—anything!

In April of '84, Davies delivered the complete recording to Capital Records. They were delighted and they immediately put out "What's Love Got to Do with It?" Meanwhile, Tina toured with Lionel Richie, singing her new songs to fans across the country. In June of '84, "Private Dancer" was released by which time "What's Love Got to Do with It?" was already climbing the charts. Things were starting to happen for Tina.

Tina became extremely popular with the fans and her record "Private Dancer" sold ten million copies around the world. Eight years after leaving Ike, Tina was back and bigger than ever.

Not very often do I allow a student to write a paper about someone he or she knows, such as a parent, a relative, or a friend. It is difficult to find research about them and students must rely primarily on interviews and any documentation the individuals possess. But in Marcy's case, I made an exception. She had worked almost every day for three years with a woman who was mentally handicapped. She knew this woman well. Below is one of her pieces, through which the reader realizes what it is like for this mentally handicapped woman to read a simple piece of text.

Ifyoucanreadthisyouaredoingwhatihavetodoeverytimeitryand readsomethingwouldyouliketospendthismuchenergyreadingal loftheprintinourworld?ididnotthinkso.

Marcy's paper contained a number of pieces in which she interpreted what it would be like to be a mentally handicapped individual. We often read about but do not live life from the perspective of such an individual. Through her paper, Marcy gave us that humbling experience.

Another genre that is very effective for including a lot of factual information in an interesting format is the resumé. Paula wrote about her idol, Martin Luther King Jr. (Figure 6–5).

Writing a resumé helps students understand all that is taken into consideration when someone applies for a job. It also gives the reader of the paper an overview of the life and accomplishments of an individual in a one-page format.

The range of topics in our multigenre papers is really incredible. When students give their oral presentations, the class can be in hysterics one minute and close to tears the next. Amy wrote her paper about chocolate. For one of her pieces, she thought it might be fun to write a singles ad for a piece of chocolate that is searching to meet another piece of candy. Here is her entry:

Personal Ads

SDCB seeks SWBB. Enjoys cool nights and shady areas. Looking for that perfect sweet to keep me company on my lonely shelf. Respond immediately. Must be shiny and have a few weeks left before expiration. Respond to Mailbox: SweetKiss

KEY:
N=Nutty D=Dark Cr=Crispy T=Truffle S=Single W=White
B=Bar Ca=Caramel C=Chocolate M=Milk BB=BonBon K=Kiss

---

23 Clinton Avenue
Atlanta, GA 87456
Martin Luther King Jr.

Objective	Co-pastor of the Ebenezer Baptist Church
Experience	1947–1954 Ebenezer Baptist Church Atlanta, GA

Assistant Minister

- Received license to preach.
- Assisted father, Reverend Martin Luther King Sr., in Sunday services.

1954–59   Dexter Avenue Baptist Church   Montgomery, AL

Pastor

- Formed the Southern Christian Leadership Conference (President).

Education   1945–1948   Morehouse College   Atlanta, GA

- Ordained as a Baptist minister.

1948–1951 Crozer Theological Seminary Chester, PA

- BA of Divinity
- Class valedictorian
- Winner of the Pearl Plafker Award for most outstanding student

1951–1955   Boston University   Boston, MA

- Ph.D. in Theology

Interests   Southern Christian Leadership Conference—President

Preaching, Striving for Freedom

FIGURE 6–5.   Resumé for Martin Luther King Jr.

Sometimes a form of writing that is easily overlooked by students is the dedication of a book. Yet almost every book has one. Here is a dedication that Jen wrote to open her paper on the Holocaust.

This book is dedicated to all those men, women, and children who endured the struggle, the pain, and the tears during those evil days. Your suffering was not in vain. We remember the Holocaust. Today, tomorrow, and forever. May you rest in peace.

Shemma Yisrael, Adonai,
Elohaynoo Adonai, Echad!

Jen's dedication was particularly appropriate for her topic. When she presented her paper to the class she ended with a brief, candle-lit prayer service in Hebrew. It was solemn and powerful.

I allowed—in fact—encouraged one student to research her grandmother for her multigenre paper. At first she had selected Disney World as her topic. After a few weeks of research, however, she found that she was losing interest in the topic. She knew that I had researched Italian immigration and was inspired to find out more about her own heritage. Her grandmother came from Poland through Ellis Island. As part of her research, Christa and her mother went to Ellis Island and found her grandmother's name inscribed in a plaque there. They visited the Statue of Liberty, and she took lots of photos. She also interviewed many family members. Christa used to spend a lot of time with her grandmother before she died and wanted to include in her multigenre paper her grandmother's recipe for potatoes.

Babchia's Famous Recipe

You will need:
  potatoes
  grease
  a pan
  potato peeler
  a knife

1. Peel potatoes.
2. Wash potatoes.
3. Cut potatoes into ¼″ slices.
4. Heat the grease.
5. Place dry potatoes into pan.
6. Let sit for a few minutes and then flip.
7. Keep flipping until golden brown and soft in the middle.

Side note: I remember every time my Babchia watched me we would make these special potatoes and play cards. Her favorite card game was called piggy. I used to love this time with her.

The motivation for topic selection varies for everyone. Patricia had an uncle who was in the Vietnam War. She felt that she didn't know him very well and thought researching the war would help her understand him better. In the following prayer, she melds some of her knowledge about the war with a refrain she heard at her church.

A LITTLE PRAYER FOR YOU

For those who left their lives behind in the name of justice.
Lord hear our prayer.
For those who encountered the bloody death of their fellow
    men.
Lord hear our prayer.
For those who were forced to kill.
Lord hear our prayer.
For those who returned home to be taunted and spat at.
Lord hear our prayer.
For those who did not come home.
Lord hear our prayer.
For those who have merely memories of a loved one.
Lord hear our prayer.
For those whose pain and suffering will never cease.
Lord hear our prayer.
For those who will never stop fighting the war within
    themselves.
Lord hear our prayer.
For those of us who can never understand.
Lord hear our prayer.

Kelly decided to research Dr. Seuss, one of her favorite authors. She designed this diploma to show us where he went to college (Figure 6–6).

Sometimes when students see a paper about a particular person they are inspired to research that person, too. Norman Rockwell surfaced two years in a row. In addition to painting the covers of the *Saturday Evening Post,* for which he is most noted, he also painted ads for many famous products. Michele got the idea of making a grocery list of these products.

A Grocery List of Norman Rockwell Ads

Adams Chewing Gum	Crest Toothpaste
Beech Nut Gum	DelMonte Fruit
Borden's Condensed Milk	Fleischmann's Yeast
Budweiser	Green Giant Niblets Corn
Campbell's Soup	Ipana Toothpaste
Carnation Evaporated Milk	Jell-O
Coca-Cola	Life Savers

DIPLOMA

THIS HEREBY CERTIFIES THAT

THEODOR SUESS GEISEL

HAS SUCCESSFULLY COMPLETED THE REQUIREMENTS
NECESSARY

FOR THE DEGREE

BACHELOR OF ARTS

IN THE STUDY OF ENGLISH AND WRITING

AT DARTMOUTH COLLEGE

ON JUNE 23, 1925

DEAN OF STUDENTS

GEORGE SMITH

DARTMOUTH COLLEGE

FIGURE 6–6.   Diploma for Dr. Seuss

Maxwell House Coffee	Quaker Oats
Nabisco Shredded Wheat	Red Rose Tea
Orange Crush	Skippy Peanut Butter
Post Cereals	Sun Maid Raisins

To make the list more appealing, Michele typed it in script and printed it on paper with a vegetable-and-fruit border.

The student work samples presented in this chapter along with the list of genres should get your students thinking about possibilities. Multigenre research papers give students freedom to express themselves in ways they feel comfortable and connect them with topics through multiple avenues. It is not only acceptable but also encouraged to take risks and see things through different eyes.

One of the ways we all take risks with our multigenre papers is to explore the arts. The first time we had our students present their papers, several of them happened to include some visuals like a poster board or a costume. We noticed how these visuals helped the students present their work and also how they were able to capture the attention of the audience. Laurie and I now require that our students integrate the fine or performing arts into their papers and/or presentations in some way. In the next chapter, I explore the arts as a way of expanding students' thinking.

EXPLORE THE ARTS
Expanding Kids' Thinking

7

Who can sit still when the rhythms of Santana pound from a CD? Who isn't moved by the intricate carving and polished surfaces of Michelangelo's *Pieta*? Who isn't amazed by the blending of humor and tragedy in Benigni's film *Life Is Beautiful*?

The arts evoke our emotions, grab our attention, and plunge us into experiences beyond our own lives. As Sylwester (1998) says, "The arts are a win-win situation. The doers and the observers both discover something about the further reaches of being human" (34).

Many of us as adults tend to be more reserved and would rather observe than produce the arts. The students in Laurie's and my classes, however, can't wait to incorporate art, music, and drama into their multigenre papers and presentations. They are young and their brains explode with creativity.

At the end of each year, I photocopy many of the multigenre papers to serve as models for the following year's students. After about a month of working with Laurie and her students, I tote these former papers to Laurie's class to share them with the children. One year, I gave a stack of papers to Margaret and Joe.

"Oh, let me see," Joe said as he flipped through the pages of a report on the space shuttle.

"Look, someone did a report on Tara Lipinski. I'm going to do mine on Michelle Kwan," Margaret said.

"Here's a neat poem," Joe said.

"I like her bumper sticker, I want to do one like this."

"This person wrote a fictional letter from Jules to his dad, John Lennon, and then put it on this cool paper with stamps around the border. Those stamps make you think that it's like a real letter."

Some reports attract attention because they provide excellent samples of a variety of writing. Others attract attention because of their physical appearance. After letting the children peruse the reports for fifteen or twenty minutes, we brainstorm ideas for their papers. One conversation went like this.

"I've got some ideas for my paper on Beethoven," Carol said. "I want to write a will about how he leaves his belongings to his relatives."

"I like the way this report shows drawings of ice skates and costumes for the Olympics," Lynn added. "I want to draw some animals that got caught in the oil spill. That way people can see how the Exxon Valdez destroyed the ocean."

"You know," I continued, "at the end of the project, students make oral presentations during which they share information about what they have learned. Some have come dressed like the people they have researched and some have props to make their presentations more interesting."

These conversations lead the children to discuss ways they can incorporate the arts to better express themselves in their papers. They also want to attract an audience's attention during their oral presentations.

"I've got this long blue-and-white madras piece of cloth. I could wrap it around my head and shoulders to make me look like I am from India when I give my talk about Gandhi," Kelly said.

"I want to make a poster with a picture of the F-117. That way I can point out how it looks and describe how it flies and attacks," Don said.

Our first day of sharing the former multigenre papers exposes the children to many ideas. Their initial thoughts about ways to make their papers and presentations appealing to others eventually will change as they get deeper into their research. Their perceptions of themselves and their goals will also change. We expect change and allow time for it to happen.

The format of traditional research reports has not changed much over the years. It is still necessary to teach this form so students can succeed in an academic setting. However, the writing and presentation skills that future workplace demands will place upon today's students now require a much more varied format. My son-in-law, who is a researcher in biochemistry, recently submitted a paper for acceptance to a scientific journal. Not only did he incorporate all kinds of figures, graphics, and tables in his article, but he also submitted a potential cover design for the journal. His article was accepted and so was his cover.

When we allow students to write in multiple genres and incorporate the fine and performing arts, we help them express their ideas in ways that tap alternative thinking processes. They now have a broad repertoire of entry points into their topics. Some children are more left-brained and are strong verbally. They read and digest material with ease and then transform their research into multiple genres. For them the arts come later, when they have finished their papers and are searching for ways to make their reports more visually attractive. Other children are more right-brained and take the opposite approach. They might begin with sketches or drawings or they might think about how they could build models. Once they create visual representations of their information they can step back and write poems, sets of directions, or obituaries.

With multigenre research, there is no prescribed format or single means of artistic expression. Each paper and its presentation are unique. This approach meets the needs of both students and teachers. This freedom of expression empowers children and forces them to think for themselves. The decisions the children make surprise and delight teachers. Teachers are no longer bored by the tedious repetition that can sometimes accompany the reading of more traditional research papers.

Decorative Papers

When students examine former multigenre research papers, one of the first things they notice is how students print their papers on colorful and appealing papers. Each year our students make their way to the local photocopy store when they are ready to produce their final drafts. Margaret purchased powder blue paper with clouds on which to print her paper about angels. Heather used paper with baby rattles, safety pins, and teddy bears to announce the birth of Mary Stevenson Cassatt. Kristina printed Elton John's top 40 hits on paper with musical staffs and notes. There are scores of different papers available. Flowers, mountain scenes, antique parchment backgrounds, or sports equipment can enhance and extend the message in a piece of writing. On the contrary, sometimes just looking at the variety of papers can inspire a piece of writing.

Many students also purchase a plastic sleeve for each piece of writing and then put the whole paper together in a three-ring binder. Lots of families and friends thumb through these papers, and the plastic sleeves preserve them.

Artwork

I encourage students to try sketching, painting, or drawing to enhance their papers. Students have used oil paints, watercolors, magic markers, crayons, artists pencils, and even finger paints to embellish their writing. Throughout her paper, Julianne used crayons to draw pictures of Dian Fossey standing before a mountain range, the outline of the continent of Africa, and pictures of *National Geographic Magazine*. She also used small ink stamps to put footprints and decorative marks around some of her pieces. Molly preferred magic markers to draw pictures of Anastasia Romanov and her family. She knew that Anastasia liked to draw pictures of flowers, so for one of her pieces she drew a picture of a young girl sitting on a bench with her cat, surrounded by a colorful landscape. Leah was an art minor and as part of her paper about Vincent van Gogh, she painted her own version of Starry Night in oils. She photographed her rendition and placed the photograph in her paper. After I showed my students how I tried to sketch Andrea Bocelli, Erin drew her interpretation of John Lennon. She admitted it was a first attempt, but we were all impressed. I've even painted a few scenes of Tuscany with a rudimentary watercolor palate. Sylwester captures one of the main reasons I now make the arts a necessary part of the multigenre papers: "Emotion, attention, and the arts aren't about the security of a correct answer, but rather about a jack-of-all-trades emotional brain that has quick, multiple, inventive solutions to most problems" (1998, 35).

Including artwork in our papers is another way for us to take risks and explore avenues in which we don't feel completely comfortable. It is also a way for us to release and express some of the emotions we feel about our topics. We are not graded or judged for our artistic efforts but instead receive praise for our attempts or success at making our papers more meaningful and interesting.

Computer Programs

Word-processing programs give students an incredible number of ways to format their pieces. As an example, Microsoft Word offers more than two hundred fonts, which can be printed in italics or bold or be underlined. Students can also manipulate the size of the print and shadow, emboss, outline, or engrave the fonts they choose. Those students who have access to color printers can vary their colors within or between pieces.

There are computer programs that will also enable students to use clip art, manipulate photos, or create original decorative pieces. One fifth grader, Claudia, worked diligently on the cover of her paper about Sacajawea. She said to me, "I made it on the computer. I took all these shapes and colored them and I kept messing up because one of the arms would be this wide and another this skinny. Finally I got it. Those fingers were really hard." Erin, who wrote about John Lennon, wanted to do something special with the lyrics from his song "Revolution." She worked for hours one night in the computer lab and finally got the lyrics to radiate in concentric circles around her piece.

Web Pages

Nicole, one of my university students, learned to create a Web page as a part of her project. Her boyfriend had signed up for AOL and as a bonus had received the opportunity to create his own Web page for free. Nicole spent long hours learning the technology and designing the Web site. She incorporated music, photos, and video clips. She even described what multigenre research was and included pieces of her paper so that those who would access her site could enjoy her writing. When she made her presentation to the class, in addition to telling us about Stevie Nicks, she brought in a computer and led us through her Web site. As part of her paper, she included a printout of the information from her Web site.

Internet Photos

The Internet is a rich source of artwork and photos. If a student is researching a famous artist such as Monet, he will be able to see copies of his work. These photos are not usually copyrighted, so they can be downloaded and printed. The student can write captions beneath each photo to help the reader understand the paper. If students have access to a color printer, these downloaded photos in combination with the colorful papers from the local printing store can really increase the visual appeal of the multigenre papers.

Students should be advised before they begin their Internet research that they should look for and gather specific photos that they feel will enhance their work.

Costumes and Memorabilia

The fifth graders and the university students love to dress up for their presentations. To deliver their talks, some students have donned the clothes their characters would have worn. Sara dressed like Annie Oakley when she discussed the sharpshooter's life and adventures. She wore a black felt cowgirl hat, bright red fringed shirt, and high cowgirl boots. Jamie proudly wore his little league uniform with a New York Yankees baseball cap for his talk on Mickey Mantle. You could tell that he was proud to play baseball and be associated with someone as great as Mantle. Margaret raised some eyebrows as she traipsed across campus dressed in the costume she designed for her multigenre presentation. She wore a silver halo, long white gloves, sheets wrapped strategically around her body, white stockings and a perfect set of silver angel wings. When she delivered her talk, we really felt we were listening to a guardian angel.

When Janine was a baby she often stayed with her grandmother. Together they would watch episodes of "I Love Lucy." Janine was hooked and has loved Lucille Ball ever since. She has collected Lucy memorabilia throughout her life and displayed some of it during her presentation. She shared posters, ceramic dishes, videos, and books. At one time, she and her sister had visited the Lucy museum, and she even had photos of their trip.

Students really respect the people they talk about in their presentations. When they wear costumes they have carefully designed or bring their personal collections to share, they demonstrate this admiration. The audience gains an understanding of their passion and thoroughly enjoys their creativity.

Drama

> Drama is problem centered, experiential, and holistic. It highlights the agency and meaning-making function of the learner. Drama is an antidote to the belief that cognition and affect, thought and feeling can and should be separated. This is because thinking, experimentation, self-perception, ethics, and feelings are always part of drama . . . Drama makes the abstract accessible and concrete. (Wilhelm and Edmiston 1998, 89)

When I read Wilhelm's quote I thought he must have been writing about multigenre research papers. They function so beautifully in the same way that drama does. When students combine multigenre papers with the use of drama and role-playing, the results are magical.

Paula chose Martin Luther King Jr. for her topic immediately. When it was time for her oral presentation, Paula wanted to inform her peers about race relations between blacks and whites back in the 1960s. At that time none of my students was even born. Paula recruited two of her male friends, one black and one white, to help her with several skits. For her opening scene she had a water fountain labeled "For Whites Only." Jallah, her black friend, walked innocently toward the fountain and took a drink.

"Hey boy, what do you think you're doing?" asked Mike, her white friend.

"I was thirsty and just wanted a drink," Jallah responded.

"Don't you know anything? You can't use that fountain. Get out of here!" Mike screamed, then he pulled Jallah from the fountain and began to beat him. The scene was brief but shocking.

Paula continued with her presentation and informed us of many of Martin Luther King's accomplishments. She also read many of her pieces. At the end of her presentation, she stepped aside and Mike entered from the right side of the classroom, singing "The Battle Hymn of the Republic" in a deep but quiet voice. Jallah came back dressed as a minister with a black shirt and a white collar. He approached the podium and bellowed with passion and emotion Martin Luther King's "I Have a Dream" speech.

Paula's was the very last multigenre presentation of the semester. It left the students speechless and some in tears.

When students engage in dramatic presentations, they have to cajole friends and family to participate. Julianne, who wrote about Dian Fossey, enlisted a student from my class to play the role of Barbara Walters for a *20/20* interview. Marcie wrote about skin cancer. She brought her mother, who had had surgery for skin cancer, to class so that she could interview her. Robin took the role of a concert announcer and brought the five Spice Girls (played by five of her friends) not only to perform for us but also to tell us about their lives.

When students include drama and role-playing in their multigenre presentations, they must plan and direct the scenes, write the scripts, and choose the costumes and props. The need to be informative drives them to write, practice, choreograph, sing, and dance. They use their interpretive and creative energies to express the passion they have for their topics. In the process they discover talents they never knew they had. It stretches their thinking.

Music

Music plays a major part in many of our presentations. Chris just started to take trumpet lessons and owned his very first instrument. He chose Louis Armstrong as his topic because he admired him so. After Chris made his presentation about Armstrong, he mustered up his courage and took his trumpet from its case. He stood before the audience and played us a song he had been practicing. The audience burst into applause. We admired him for his courage.

Sandra carried her boom box and placed it next to her in the front of the class. She had made a medley of Paul Simon songs to demonstrate the different types of music he had written over the years. Excerpts from his albums *Bridge Over Troubled Waters, Rhythm of the Saints,* and *Capeman* gave us a taste of the genius of this singer and songwriter. It is hard to keep still when the lyrics and rhythms of "Me and Julio Down by the School-yard" rock the classroom.

Sometimes students who you think are quiet will surprise you. When Kelly finished her presentation about Tina Turner, she stepped out from behind the podium, put on a blond, wild wig, and lip-synched Tina's version of "Proud Mary."

With most presentations it is easy to see how music can create an ambiance, give the audience a demonstration of a performer's musical talents, or help students slip inside the skin of a character. If you refer to the list of topics we have researched over the last four years (see Chapter 3), you can see that music could be used in a number of creative ways for almost any one of them.

Commercial Videos

Videos are a major part of our culture. There are multiple video stores in every neighborhood. We also have access over the Internet to purchase videos on almost any topic imaginable. In addition, most libraries let users borrow videos for free. It makes sense for students to consider the power of video in their presentations.

Students have used clips from a documentary about Jacques Cousteau, scenes from *My Fair Lady,* episodes from the Ed Sullivan Show, and clips from some of John Travolta's movies to entertain all of us. When doing my paper on immigration, I found a few-minute clip at the beginning of *God-father II* that helped me show what conditions were like on Ellis Island. Laurie and I allow our students to include brief video segments in their presentations if it really helps them convey their messages.

Student-Designed Videos

As part of their presentations, some students make their own videos. Caila chose Giovanni Boccaccio as her topic and enlisted her parents to dress up and play the roles of Giovanni and his wife. Caila played the role of the reporter and captured scenes at their home and eventually at the graveyard where Boccaccio was buried.

Suzanne was a theater minor and was always busy with productions. As part of her presentation on the history of the Broadway musical, she not only presented clips from many famous musicals but also shared clips of herself singing in several productions. Many times we don't know all the talents that our students possess. It can be a nice surprise.

Crafts

Some students integrate their hobbies with their presentations. Glenn wrote his paper on King Francis I and decided that he wanted to create the family crest. First he carved the crest and then painted it gray with black letters.

Mary Ellen wrote her paper on the musical group Queen. She told me she had collected Queen memorabilia since eighth grade and had been waiting for an assignment like the multigenre paper her whole life. For her creative piece, Mary Ellen decided to design and craft a needlepoint picture of Freddie Mercury, the lead singer of Queen. When she completed it she matted it with a border of musical notes and had it framed. She surprised herself with the number of hours she spent on the needlepoint. We were all surprised by the painstaking detail she used to capture such an uncanny resemblance.

Christina found a unique way to submit her paper about Joan of Arc. She was completely immersed in the life of this heroic woman. Instead of the traditional three-ring binder, Christina decided to print out her paper and sew the sheets of paper to a long brocade banner. She wound the banner on a wooden dowel. Just as Joan of Arc would go into battle with her banner, Christina made her presentation carrying her banner to the front of the class.

Demonstrations and Models

When students write their papers about sports figures, they really have a passion for the topics. A student usually plays the same sport and knows quite a bit about it. He or she is developing expertise and often aspires to be just like the person he or she is writing about. After Michele made her presentation about the gymnast Mary Lou Retton, she demonstrated a cartwheel, roundoff, and walkover. Melanie was an avid volleyball player, and, as part of her presentation on Gabbie Reese, she brought in her volleyball and explained how to serve, spike, and dig.

Cameron decided to do his paper on Leonardo da Vinci. He was intrigued by the many drawings and models this Renaissance scientist and artist had created. As part of his project, he decided to construct his own models. Using tissue paper and balsa wood, he copied Leonardo's flying machine and parachute.

Travis wrote his multigenre paper about the Alamo. He drew maps of the attack plan and also made a plaster of Paris model of the Alamo. Using the maps and the model, he could describe the Battle of the Alamo with ease.

Using demonstrations and models facilitates students' oral presentations. It gets them away from using note cards. They focus their energies instead upon the process of doing something they know well or describing something they have created. They speak with confidence.

Artificial Artifacts

If students are not able to secure real artifacts to bring to their multigenre oral presentations, they create their own. In her talk about the impressionist painter Mary Cassatt, Heather decided to have audience members participate in an art auction. She gave students Popsicle sticks with numbers attached that they could use for bidding. She also gave students Monopoly money to use for the process. She purchased postcards of many of Cassatt's famous paintings and as she held each up, she described it. She gave each postcard to the highest bidder. As part of her research she also went to the Boston Museum of Fine Arts to see the visiting Cassatt exhibition. While there, she picked up brochures about Cassatt's work for everyone in the class. We all felt very much a part of the art world by the time she finished her presentation.

Probably one of the most humorous of all the presentations was Amy's report on John Gotti, the reputed mobster. She explained to us that she had always been interested in the mob and particularly in Gotti. She had the class convinced that as part of her research she had sent a letter to Gotti in jail, where he is serving time. She told us he wrote back. To prove it, she brought his letter, addressed to her, to class. She opened the envelope and pulled out a long sheet of toilet paper on which "Gotti" had answered her questions from his cell. It took a few seconds before most of the class realized the letter was a hoax. Her creativity really did catch us off guard and we enjoyed a good laugh together.

Posters

At the end of the multigenre project, Laurie and her students come to the university to make their presentations during a night of celebration with family and friends. Following those presentations, we all gather in a large ballroom in our administration building to display the students' work. Laurie requires all her students to design and display posters or backboards to accompany their papers and serve as visuals.

As an example, Molly wrote her paper on Anastasia Romanov, daughter of Nicholas II, tsar of Russia. She constructed a trifold backboard, which she covered with red and black solid and calico fabrics. She topped each section with a pointed gold dome to represent the architecture of many of the buildings in Russia. She downloaded photos of the Romanov family and backed each with colored construction paper. She added a caption beneath each photo and mounted them all on the backboard. She displayed her backboard on a table and placed her report in front of it.

Dioramas

For her artistic piece about Denmark and the Holocaust, Emma lined a shoebox with black construction paper. She dotted the sky with twinkling golden stars and a crescent moon. She placed a ship being splashed by waves in the foreground. Inside the ship were the Jews escaping from Denmark to Sweden during the Holocaust.

In her diorama, Claudia constructed a small boat holding Lewis and Clark, with Sacajawea standing in the bow. Behind them were mountains and a pale blue sky with white clouds. Sacajawea was proudly leading the expedition.

Lottie used her imagination when she created a diorama about Amelia Earhart. She titled it "My Diorama of Where Amelia Earhart Might Have Crashed." She depicted the Howland Islands with Amelia's brown plane crashed into a rock. She added a yellow plane with a patrol searching for traces of her. Amelia had a small camp in the diorama and there were even sharks swimming in the water. Lottie mixed fact and fiction and had a great time doing it.

Photography

The photographs of William Wegman and Ann Geddes have inspired a number of multigenre research papers. Wegman photographs weimaraners (dogs) dressed like humans in everyday situations while Geddes photographs babies in natural settings often as a variety of flowers, vegetables, and insects.

The first year we explored multigenre research papers, Amy decided to write about Wegman because she loved his work but also because she had two weimaraners of her own. As part of her paper, she decided to photograph her own dogs, Lily and Max. She used their photos to illustrate a children's book she designed as one of her genres. She caught Lily and Max eating breakfast, lounging, hiding from her to avoid work, refusing to wear the outfits she wanted, and playing ball together at the end of the shoot.

In a subsequent year, Anna chose Ann Geddes because Anna was interested in photography herself. She had taken photography classes and when it was time for her to make her presentation, she shared many of her own black-and-white photos that she had taken around campus. Anna also tried to emulate Geddes by photographing her own little nephew dressed in costume. She admitted it was not as easy at it looked.

In both Amy's and Anna's cases it didn't matter that their photos were far from the quality of Wegman's and Geddes'. What did matter was that they were inspired by their research and understanding of their topics to want to stretch themselves toward that goal and really become one with their topics.

The Melding of the Arts and Multigenre

When students meld the arts with their multigenre papers and presentations, they sharpen and extend their thinking in new directions. They grasp tiny details from their research and expand upon them. They take their new-found knowledge and communicate it more fully. They possess an increased awareness of their world and they share this gift with the rest of us.

Once students have written all their genres and completed their artistic pieces, they need to concentrate on ways to tie their whole papers together. In the next chapter, I explore some ways to make student papers understandable and enjoyable to their readers.

8 CREATE FLOW
Pulling It All Together

I can remember writing traditional research papers in college. I'd work on one for several months and when I finally finished, I'd place it in a clear plastic binder and turn it in to the professor as quickly as possible—and, I might add, with a great sigh of relief.

Once multigenre papers are written, however, students do not slap them into binders and turn them in to the teacher. There is still a responsibility to the reader that students must address, and they sense this. Tom Romano writes, "Multigenre papers require a great deal of readers. So much is implicit, so little explicit that multigenre papers can be quite a cognitive load" (2000, 149). Because so much is implicit, you have to help students think about ways to present their pieces. You have to help them bring coherence, or flow, to a paper that might contain many disparate elements. You can begin by breaking the class into small groups and asking for a volunteer from each group who is willing serve as a discussion leader and use his or her paper as the center of that discussion. Here is a list of questions that the discussion leader can use to get the group started:

1. Do any of you have any previous knowledge about my topic?
2. What would you want or have to know about my topic before you read my paper?
3. When you read my pieces, which ones can stand alone and be self-explanatory?
4. If I place all my pieces on a table, will you help me decide which should come first, second, and third?
5. Can someone record the different ways we chose and why?
6. What ways can you think of that could help the readers of multigenre papers move from piece to piece or make connections between pieces?

After the small-group discussions, get back together and have each group report the various ways it thought about to create flow within papers. When you have finished the discussion, you can share the ways my university students suggested, which I describe here. Your students will probably gener-

ate many of the same suggestions and more. It is best if you let them think
the problem through on their own before they rely on others.

97

Create Flow

Techniques to Link Genres and Create Flow
Chronological Order

For those with very logical minds, organizing the paper into chronological
order makes sense. A student can begin with a birth certificate, which
announces the names of the parents, place and time of birth, and the person's full name. It is a concise way to open the paper. These papers then
follow the person through his or her life, usually include photos from stages
in his or her life, and are meshed with appropriate genres along the way.
This type of paper usually ends with an obituary or a tribute.

Stanzas and Lyrics

Sometimes a student can make connections among the pieces in his paper
by dividing a poem up into stanzas or natural breaks and including one segment after each section of his paper. If the poem is well known, the reader
will realize that only a portion of the poem is presented and will be antic-
ipating the next stanza further on in the paper. If the student has written
the poem himself, he might want to include lines of repetition that will
show up throughout the paper, serving as transitions between pieces.

Students can also use lyrics from famous songs to unite pieces of their
papers. They can break up entire songs or rely on the refrains to link sections.

"Dear Reader" Letters

Sometimes students feel the need to talk directly to the readers of their
papers before the readers begin. In this case, the student can open her paper
with a "Dear Reader" letter. In it she can provide background information,
facts about individual pieces, or an invitation for readers to participate in
the multigenre experience.

Diary or Journal Entries

A simple but effective way to connect pieces within the multigenre paper
is through diary or journal entries. After research pieces, newspaper articles,
or essays, a student can slip in journal entries written from the perspective
of the famous or historical figure. These diary and journal entries help readers feel they have a personal connection to that person's life and that they
are part of that person's confidence.

Interviews

Another technique to unify the paper is to use an interview. Have the student begin the interview and ask about a certain aspect of the person's life.
Once the person responds, the student can then elaborate upon the response
through poetry, ads, or any appropriate form of writing. Later on in the

paper, the interview can continue. Then the student should follow up once more with further genres that illustrate the new information.

Divided Research Pieces

A related idea is to have students divide their research pieces into natural breaks, then follow each section with appropriate genres and pieces of art.

Table of Contents

Some students want the reader to get the complete overview of the genres upfront. These students write tables of contents that supply the background information and set up the readers to more readily use interpretive skills when they reach each piece.

Opening Research Piece

Similar to creating a table of contents is leading with the entire research piece. It familiarizes the reader with the facts about the person or event and builds her background knowledge. The writer has to trust that this introduction will be evidence enough for the reader to make connections and read between the lines or genres in the remainder of the paper.

Genre Sections

Some students like to place dividers in their multigenre papers. They label each section with a title such as poetry, short story, and photographs. This is most helpful if the reader is interested in analyzing writing rather than viewing the paper as a whole.

Artistic Connections

Students can tie their papers together by using recurring decorative motifs or papers. The visuals set a tone and create a mood that repeats throughout. Soft pastels might be appropriate for a paper about Jackie Kennedy and brightly colored sports designs can enhance papers about Michael Jordan. Also, a series of photos strategically placed can carry a theme throughout.

Oral Presentations

If students are going to make oral presentations at the end of the project, they can rely heavily upon these presentations to acquaint the teacher, classmates, and other readers of the papers about how and why they wrote what they did. So many times the oral presentations set the background information for the audience, who will read the papers after the presentations. The presenters take the opportunity to explain any aspects of the project they choose to highlight. They might discuss why they chose their topics, how they selected their genres, what difficulties they might have had with writing, or what they have learned because of the project.

During their presentations they also introduce time lines, photos, paintings, models, costumes, music, or skits that they use as springboards to reading various pieces from their papers. At this time they explain why they chose each piece of artistic expression and how it ties to the genres they read to the audience. The oral presentations give them the chance to say all that might not be said in the paper. Having students give oral presentations really is one of the most effective ways to tie the entire project together. In the next chapter, I explain how to prepare students to give their oral presentations for their peers, parents, and teachers.

9 SPEAK UP

Recognizing the Power of Oral Communication

> The quality of life is enriched when individuals choose to engage in ethical, constructive, self-aware communication with their families, friends, co-workers, neighbors, and fellow community members. (Chaney and Burk 1998, 7)

People talk all the time. Kids ice-skating on the pond on Saturday afternoon chat about the movie they saw the night before. Children ask questions at school to clarify the meaning of a chapter they have just read in science. Software designers discuss ways to make programs to help people complete their taxes. The president of the Unites States delivers the State of the Union Address. We need to communicate to function in society. Oral communication is used all the time for personal, social, educational, occupational, and civic purposes. But is it used effectively? Lack of clear oral communication can cause children to fail in school, can damage self-esteem, can cause violence among coworkers, and can even cause wars among nations. Students need to learn how to use language appropriately and how to deliver their messages in a way that will reach their intended audience.

Right from our first year working together on the multigenre papers, Laurie and I believed that our students should work toward a culminating activity that would allow them to extend their reading and writing skills into the realm of listening and speaking. Most adults don't feel comfortable speaking before a crowd. We can't expect children to, either. They need to work toward it gradually and build confidence along the way. We must start small and give them authentic contexts in which to operate.

Students Take a First Step

Laurie introduces her students to their first oral presentation in the fall. They begin with a casual discussion of what makes a good speech. One class decided that speakers should know their information, should look at their audience, and should not fill the speech with "ums" and "you knows." They decided that they would rate their speeches on a scale from strongest (4) to weakest (1). They used this scale because it is how their report cards were designed and they were familiar with it.

Laurie then presented her children with the task. She required each of them to read a children's book—no chapter books allowed—and to get up before his or her peers to describe the problem, solution, and events that led up to that solution. Laurie explained she would videotape their presentations and they would later rate them with their four-point scale.

Mary was the first to present. She placed a large poster on the chalkboard sill. It had a royal blue background and cutout figures of a circus tent, a barn, a car, a bright yellow sunshine, and a big red dog.

In front of Mary there was a long table covered with a bright red cloth. Behind the table were four of Mary's friends on their knees with hand puppets. Mary stood at the chalkboard and introduced her book. "The book I read is called *Clifford Gets a Job* (1985) by Norman Birdwell," she began. "One day Emily and Clifford, the big red dog, hear Emily's mother and father talking about how much it costs to feed Clifford. They don't know if they can afford it. So Clifford decides he must get a job. First he goes to the circus and talks with the ringmaster."

Up popped the hand puppets of Clifford and the ringmaster. They were made of felt and each was two-sided. On one side was a smiling character and on the other side a frowning one. As Mary continued to describe the events of the story, the puppets interacted and flipped back and forth between happy and sad.

Mary did not use any note cards because between the puppets and her poster she was able to retell the sequence of events. Clifford failed at his circus job and at a job he got on a farm. He finally found success chasing robbers for the police. For this he was hired permanently and for his pay he was fed plenty of dog food. The problem was solved. Mary faltered a few times during her talk but regained her composure. She did a nice job for her first attempt before her peers.

Because the books the children choose contain simple plots, the content and reading are easy. The children can focus their efforts primarily on their oral presentations. There is not a lot of information to relate, so they can deliver it without relying on note cards. They can use their creativity to construct the props to help them remember what they want to say. Later, when they do the oral presentations about their multigenre topics, they will be challenged to deliver more difficult content through more sophisticated talks. But as a first task, Laurie gives her students a very simple assignment, thus setting them up for initial success.

Students Analyze Their Presentations

When all the presentations are complete, Laurie sets up a TV and VCR in a coatroom that is adjacent to her classroom. She posts a schedule so the children can slip into the coatroom and individually view and rate themselves while she still conducts class. They watch themselves and on a note card rate themselves from 4 to 1. Laurie says that inevitably they are more critical of themselves than she would ever be.

Students Create Their Own Rubrics

Kids are bright and they know a good presentation when they see one. Rather than give them the answers, we think it's best for them to do as much discovery on their own as possible. Every year we have videotaped our student presentations so we have a large repertoire of good and not-so-strong speeches from which to choose for demonstration purposes. Since you will be just beginning this multigenre project, you might not have tapes available. A segment from the Weather Channel or the nightly news will give your students professional speakers to analyze. Segments of programs from local access TV will provide examples of more "regular" people in action.

In April, Laurie shows her children six tapes of former students giving their oral presentations. The children watch intently because they know this is something they will be required to do in another three weeks. Then Laurie breaks her students into groups of four and assigns them a task. She tells them, "I want you to construct a rubric for oral presentations. You should decide what a person would have to do to receive a 4, 3, 2, or 1. Select one person from your group to be the recorder and divide your paper into four blocks headed by the numbers 1 through 4. Write the behaviors for each category under each section. You have 10 minutes."

The children scatter to all areas of the classroom and get to work. They have worked with rubrics before. I can overhear their conversations as I move between groups. They often sound like this:

"I think we should put that they have to have lots of good information. Remember that kid we saw, he didn't seem to know much."

"Yea, I didn't like the way he talked into his paper. Maybe we should put that down under 1."

Although there is a designated note taker, all the children have notebooks and are busy writing. They are on task and before we know it, their time is up. One class had the following discussion:

"OK," Laurie said. "Let's begin with a 4. I'll write your responses. Someone from Emma's group."

"They should know their info by heart."

"Andrew, how about you?"

"They should speak clearly."

"Someone from Claudia's group."

"They should make eye contact and be creative."

"What do you mean by creative, can you expand on that?"

The children continued to dictate and Laurie managed to call on each child in the class. It was fast-paced and the children were eager to contribute their ideas. They finalized their criteria and Laurie asked Claudia to copy it. Here is that class' final list of competencies:

4

knows information by heart
speaks clearly
makes eye contact
is organized and presents material in sequential order
has a good interest builder
keeps talk to 5–7 minutes

3

does not read a lot
knows most of the information
says "um" sometimes but not too much
sometimes makes eye contact

2

not enough information
mumbles
talks too fast or too slow
talks too quietly
little eye contact
nervous distractions

1

little information and appears disinterested
reads too much
no eye contact
too many nervous distractions
strays from topic/lack of sequence
says "like" and "um" too much
too long or too short

These children did a pretty good job. Next Laurie gave them the chance to apply their newly designed rubrics.

"Now I'm going to show you a videotape of three children presenting their multigenre papers and I want you to rate them. I will be also be asking you why you rated them this way. Here's speaker number one."

The children watched with interest and some jotted notes. Laurie fast-forwarded the tape partway into the second speaker's presentation because she speaks for fifteen minutes. When the third speaker finished, Laurie called on her students once again.

"Brian, what did you give speaker number one?"

"I thought he deserved a 1."

"How about you, Andrew?"

"I thought he should get a 2."

"John, how about you?"

"I thought a 3."

Laurie took a vote and determined that most of the children thought speaker one should get a 2. They could see the diversity of response, however.

"OK, how about speaker two? But this time tell me how you rated her and the reasons for your rating."

Daniel began, "I gave her a 2 because she mumbled and had lots of nervous distractions. Her speech was too long. She didn't have much eye contact, either."

"Well, I gave her a 3," Emma said, because she used sarcasm and I like that. It spiced up her talk. She did read too much, though."

"I thought she should get a 1," Mike said. "I couldn't understand her and I didn't even know what her topic was."

Laurie asked about speaker three. Brian volunteered. "He was the worst. I gave him a 1. He never looked up, he repeated words, he didn't know his topic and he read from his paper. I wouldn't have known his topic if he didn't have that poster in the background. Oh yea, and he didn't speak clearly, either."

John raised his hand and added some redeeming value to speaker three's report. "I couldn't understand what he said and he did look at his paper. It looked like he didn't know his topic but you could see from his report that he put a lot of hard work into it. He did get better at the end. He was probably scared and shy. He did have good effort."

Laurie praised her children: "You have done a super job. Give yourself a hand." The children applauded. Laurie continued, "You see it's not easy to rate someone. You all have slightly different opinions. Overall, do you know what you have to aim for to get a 4?"

"Yes," they all chimed in in unison.

"And a 3?"

"Yes!"

"Let hope we don't aim for 2s and 1s."

Although all their rubrics are not perfect, the children have a good sense of what is expected of them. Through discussion and application they internalize the rubrics they have created. The children place their rubrics in their Resource Notebooks for future reference.

A Rating Scale Prompts Discussion

Once the children have developed their own rubrics, I give them a copy of the following oral critique form that the university students use to rate their own performances. It was originally designed by Julia Mahon, a professor in the Department of Education. We have discussed and modified it each year to suit the needs of the group. The form incorporates all that the children have discussed and also allows degrees of performance to be measured. Eventually, after the children present their multigenre projects before their families and friends at the university, Laurie has each of them complete this form for self-evaluation.

CRITIQUE FORM FOR ORAL COMMUNICATIONS SKILLS

NAME: _____ TOPIC: _____

4=EXEMPLARY, 3=ABOVE AVERAGE, 2=AVERAGE, 1=NEEDS IMPROVEMENT

VERBAL COMMUNICATION SKILLS

Language is vivid, clear, and appropriate	4	3	2	1
Vocal variety and enthusiasm	4	3	2	1
Appropriate rate of speech	4	3	2	1
Appropriate volume	4	3	2	1
Appropriate pitch	4	3	2	1
Clear enunciation (endings, *ing, ts, ds* . . .)	4	3	2	1
Fluency (not breaking up with "you know," "like," "a," "um")	4	3	2	1

NONVERBAL COMMUNICATION SKILLS

Eye contact	4	3	2	1
Appropriate nonverbal gestures	4	3	2	1

TOPIC PRESENTATION

Introduces self and topic clearly	4	3	2	1
Presents information logically	4	3	2	1
Demonstrates passion for topic	4	3	2	1
Concludes topic appropriately	4	3	2	1
Uses time effectively	4	3	2	1
Use of visual/audio/multimedia aids	4	3	2	1

BEST PART OF PRESENTATION:

AREAS THAT NEED IMPROVEMENT:

FIGURE 9–1. Critique Form for Oral Communications Skills

We discuss each of the major areas on the critique sheet and develop several lists of tips that will help the children with the preparation and practice of their presentations.

Verbal Communication Skills

- Use language to fit your audience; don't use slang like "awesome" and "cool."
- Speak slowly and naturally and don't use a monotone voice.
- Speak loud enough for people in the back of the room to hear you.
- Don't chop off the endings to your words.
- Don't use "like" and "um" (those are the worst offenders).

Nonverbal Communication Skills

- Look at the audience and not at your paper.
- Use note cards rather than a written-out speech.
- Avoid standing at a podium, at least part of the time.
- Look at the space you have and move about within that space.
- Set your props up ahead of time and be sure to use all of them in sequence.
- Keep your hands folded or hold your props, don't wave your hands around or twist your hair.

Topic Presentation

- Open your talk with an attention getter like a quote, a question, or a brief story.
- Work through your talk in a logical sequence by writing highlights on cards, and integrate your arts and media throughout the presentation.
- Keep a watch handy to keep track of your time.
- Keep your enthusiasm level up throughout the whole presentation.
- End with a summary of your key points; don't just say, "That's it."

Students Present to Their Peers

By mid-April, Laurie's students have made their oral presentations about children's books, analyzed their performances, watched the presentations of previous students, developed their own rubrics, rated other speakers, and reviewed the university critique sheet. They have completed the writing of their multigenre papers and prepared their creative arts pieces. Their next step is to move beyond their own class and present to other children in their school. There are three fifth-grade classrooms in Laurie's school, so she divides her children into two groups and has each group present its speeches to one of the other two fifth grades. This takes place during the children's language arts period. Laurie videotapes them once again so that they can see themselves one last time before they present at the university.

One year, Jimmy was among the first to present his multigenre paper, about Lou Gehrig. He began by saying, "I did my paper on Lou Gehrig, the famous baseball player. Lou Gehrig was born on June 19, 1930, in New York City. His parents were poor German immigrants. Lou was the only one of four children to survive infancy. Many kids of the poverty level of the Gehrigs never exceeded eighth grade because they went to work. His mother insisted that he go to the High School of Commerce."

Jimmy continued and explained that Lou played football and baseball, that he got a scholarship to Columbia, and that eventually the New York Yankees signed him. He informed us about Lou's close relationship with Babe Ruth and his eventual visit to the Mayo Clinic, where doctors informed him he was suffering from amyotrophic lateral sclerosis (ALS). Jimmy finished his research piece by saying, "Lou said he was the luckiest man on earth for his remarkable career and all the friends he had made while playing baseball. Lou Gehrig died at the age of 37 on June 2, 1941." Then Jimmy shared a birth certificate, an award congratulating Lou for playing 2,130 games in a row, an invitation from Babe Ruth to a party in Lou's honor, and several other pieces. At the end of his presentation, Jimmy showed the class a baseball signed by famous baseball players. They had all signed it in Lou's honor. Jimmy admitted the ball was something he made, but the kids were impressed with his creativity.

The children applauded and asked several questions. Following each student's presentation, the children in the audience completed this simple evaluation form:

MULTIGENRE RESEARCH PAPER PRESENTATIONS

NAME _____

TOPIC _____

PLEASE DESCRIBE THE BEST PARTS OF THIS PRESENTATION

PLEASE DESCRIBE HOW THIS PRESENTATION COULD BE IMPROVED

We collected the forms and gave them to each presenter. Here are some of the children's comments about Jimmy.

The Best Parts of This Presentation
- How you told about his childhood and I liked your baseball. I liked how you had important props, very interesting.

- Told how he grew up and about the scout.
- That Ruth and Lou were teammates.
- How he got into professional baseball.
- Loud and clear voice and very interesting topic. Told only the necessary facts.
- The interview was one of the best parts he read.
- I liked how Lou was so interested in school.

How This Presentation Could Be Improved

- You could have told more about Lou and Ruth.
- You read too much.
- Tell more about his family.
- Talk slower.
- Tell how he died and speak clearly. Tell more about the disease.

The forms always contain some positive aspects about the presentations and usually have some suggestions for improvement. I find that the fifth graders are often more candid with their suggestions for improvement than my college students are when they present to their peers.

Students Present to a Wider Audience

During the last week of our project, Laurie and I always bring her children to the university for what we call a night of Multigenre Madness. For the children, it is probably the most challenging and important moment of the whole semester. As Laurie says, "It is where they find out they can do it." The children present the results of their research to an audience of parents, relatives, friends, teachers, principals, and university students. Multigenre Madness gives the children a second chance to visit the campus and it brings them into an atmosphere that gives them a sense of importance. It tells them, "We value what you are about to do."

The last time we held Multigenre Madness, Lesley Faria and Landa Patterson, two teachers from the nearby Pennfield School, also joined us. They, along with half of my students, had conducted multigenre research projects with their fourth and fifth graders. The children from Pennfield School and Laurie's fifth graders from Cranston Calvert had already met once when they all came to the university to conduct research for their multigenre papers.

We planned Multigenre Madness for 6:00 P.M. so that relatives and friends could attend after work. We sent home invitations along with maps of the buildings and parking areas at the university. Parents and my students offered to bake goodies for the celebration. We surveyed the children to get a rough estimate of the total number of people who might attend the celebration. We were more than two hundred strong!

I reserved eight university classrooms and arranged a videocamera to be set up in each. Since the university doesn't own eight videocameras, some parents volunteered to bring their videocameras and tape the children presenting in the rooms where their children would present. We wanted the tapes so that the children could view their final presentations and so that we would have more sample tapes to share with our future students.

We divided the children into eight groups and made sure that there was a mixture of Cranston Calvert and Pennfield students and their families in each. In some rooms, the children were scheduled to present to more than twenty-five people.

I also reserved the ballroom of our university's administration building and had long tables set up. When the children completed their oral presentations in the university classrooms, they had to carry their props, backboards, and reports to the ballroom and place them on the tables. This gave everyone a chance to view and discuss all the projects, not just the ones they saw presented in their individual classrooms.

The Audience Responds
At the end of the presentations, we distributed the following questionnaire to get feedback from members of the audience.

MULTIGENRE RESEARCH QUESTIONNAIRE

1. What did your child learn through the multigenre experience?

2. What did you enjoy most about the children's presentations?

Comments or suggestions:

Here is what some folks had to say about what their children had learned through the multigenre experience:

My child learned how to cooperate with a variety of individuals. She learned a lot about her chosen topic but probably more importantly, she learned to *communicate* what she learned.

My daughter learned a *huge* amount about the Renaissance period (her parents did too!).

My daughter learned how to do research and to organize. She also learned to believe in her ability to complete the project and speak to an audience.

My son learned how to work independently, he gained computer experience with word processing and the Internet, and he learned the importance of editing.

Here are some things the audience members said they enjoyed about the oral presentations:

> Their obvious love for their topics.
>
> The fact that she was able to get up in front of people and do this. I am very proud!
>
> How much they all seemed to enjoy the process.
>
> The enthusiasm and originality. It was great.
>
> Hearing kids present interesting information in a fun, professional forum.
>
> They all set high standards and met them. They were courageous when presenting.

The children *were* courageous. They had brought their multigenre projects to fruition. They had started by summarizing simple children's books and presenting them to their class and had ended by presenting the results of their three-month multigenre research projects. They had learned a lot about oral presentations.

The evening of Multigenre Madness marks the end of our semester-long collaboration. It is a time for celebration and evaluation. Evaluation is important throughout the project because it is so performance-based. It is also important at the end of the project when we can take a look at the experience as a whole. In the next chapter I review all the formative and summative evaluation methods we use throughout our project.

THE BIG PICTURE 10
Evaluating the Projects

It's twenty of nine in the morning and the phone rings.

"Hello," I say as I pick up. "Oh, Don, you are early. I didn't expect your call until nine."

"I hit a block in my writing and I can't go on; I need a conference."

"OK, what are you writing?"

"I'm trying to write a chapter about how people in the state of Maine work so well together to solve problems with the teaching of reading in their district. They energize each other. They simply go to places where the teaching of reading is successful and ask, 'How did you do it?'"

"So what's the block?"

"Well, I have interviewed this one woman from Maine who does incredible work, reads everything in sight, and works with four different schools. What she does is amazing."

"So how does this relate to the Maine chapter?"

"She really needs her own chapter because of the importance of her work but if I do that I'm not sure how I should restructure what I want to say about Maine."

We begin to think. He could break the chapter on Maine into smaller segments and fit it into different chapters, or he could highlight Maine and other school districts throughout the United States that have ideas that really work. Our chat helps him review his thoughts, brainstorm ideas, and set new direction.

Likewise, I send Don chapters I am writing all the time. We set times for brief conferences over the phone. He always starts with some positive aspects and then asks questions. I jot notes in the margins and then return to my writing. Sometimes it is easy to revise. Sometimes our conversations open more difficult paths that I have to contemplate for several days before anything surfaces. We call each other because we want someone to help us assess where we are and where we want to go. We want to evaluate what we have accomplished to date. We need direction and encouragement to move ahead. We want feedback and the chance to get recharged.

As Jane Hansen (1998) says in *When Learners Evaluate,* "Evaluation is the act of finding value in someone or something" (1). When Don and

I chat, we listen to each other. We value what we have done and what we are trying to do. As teachers we need to find value in what our students are trying to do, but more importantly, we need to help them learn to find value in their own work. To accomplish this we must slow down, include them, and listen to what they have to say.

Sometimes it is difficult to listen. We want to cover the curriculum. We create assignments, tell students exactly how they should be done, evaluate them, and assign grades—bang! Then we repeat the cycle. This leaves students little voice and little opportunity to learn about evaluating themselves and their progress.

Good evaluation leads to good teaching and learning. Laurie and I believe that if we want to enhance our students' performance, we cannot rely solely on summative evaluation; we must plan a number of formative evaluation experiences along the way. We also believe that for evaluation to be good, we need to include our students in the process whenever possible.

As Jane Hansen says,

Evaluation starts with the learners. When we start to ask for our students' evaluations, they often surprise us, and we realize how far we might have gone astray without their insights. Their thoughts beget our teaching and then we have to ask them, again, what they think. They evaluate. We revise what we do, and, eventually, we find ourselves in a teaching situation that can't exist without the frequent evaluations of students. We thirst for their insights. (1998, 1–2)

In this chapter I describe the many tools Laurie and I use to evaluate our students, the ways they evaluate themselves, and the ways outsiders evaluate them. I have discussed many of these more fully in previous chapters, so I reference those chapters for your ease of review. I describe other methods of evaluation for the first time in this chapter.

Questions to Get Started

Before you can decide what evaluation schemes to use with the multigenre project, you should consider the following questions.

- Which standards or curriculum goals do I hope to meet through this project?
- What knowledge, skills, and attitudes do I hope students will achieve by the end of the project?
- How long do I think I would like my students to work on this project?
- What types of evaluation tools can I use to measure these goals?
- What forms of evaluation can I use to ensure both formative and summative evaluation?

- At what times do I want to introduce the various forms of evaluation?
- Am I including some evaluation tools that require student input?

Videotaped Oral Presentation (Chapter 9)

Laurie introduces her students to their first oral presentation in October by having them each read a simple children's book. Using props, they retell the stories for their peers. Laurie videotapes the presentations. The children informally discuss what constitutes a good presentation. Then they individually review their performances. They rate themselves on a scale of 4 (best) to 1 (worst) on index cards and give the cards to Laurie. She says they are always more critical than she would be. It is a good beginning to self-evaluation.

Literacy Survey (Chapter 2)

We use the Literacy Survey as a pre- and postevaluation. It reveals students' perceptions of themselves as readers and writers. It also gives us an overview of their attitudes toward literacy. Some of my students have made dramatic shifts from feeling negatively toward reading and writing to becoming literacy proponents by the end of the project.

Student Resource Notebooks (Chapter 2)

Laurie has the children construct their Resource Notebooks at the beginning of the project. They are composed of three parts: a section with samples of the most common forms of writing, a section where all rough drafts of the paper are kept, and a section where all notes, note cards, and downloaded information from the Internet are kept. These notebooks keep the children's work organized and let them keep track of their progress. Laurie can also evaluate the children's progress by periodically collecting the notebooks.

Student Response Journals (Chapter 2)

Laurie has the children write in their blue books at the end of each Tuesday's session. They are to answer three questions: (1) What did you accomplish today? (2) How do you feel about it? and (3) What questions do you have at this time? Laurie responds to each child each week. She gives them words of encouragement and answers their questions. These response journals also serve as records of weekly progress.

Student Process Journals (Chapter 2)

Students in the upper grades can keep process journals. These journals are like logs where students write the date and what they do each day they work on their projects. These entries can include such things as researching at the library, writing, making outlines, taking notes, constructing their creative pieces, or typing their reports. This informs the teacher about the students' thought processes and organizational strategies.

Assignment Sheets

When we first began the project, Laurie and I found that simply telling the children to work on their papers for the next week was too unstructured. Now we have each child complete the following form at the end of every Tuesday's session. They have to analyze what they have accomplished to date and determine what they will work on during the upcoming week. Then they sign them, saying that they agree to follow through. This places responsibility on them to set their own academic purposes. Students keep these assignment sheets in their Resource Notebooks.

Assignment Sheet

Child's Name:

Assignment:

Date Due:

Additional Comments:

Signature: _____

K–W–L (Chapter 3)

By February, the children have selected their topics. Next they need to evaluate their prior knowledge of the subject (K). Then they have to think about what they want to find out when they start their research (W). This again places the evaluation responsibility on the students. When they finish their papers, they can complete the (L) section of their K–W–L charts with what they have learned.

Preparation for the Visit to the University Library (Chapter 3)

In February, Laurie's students visit the university library. Between their K–W–Ls and the information they might have already acquired from working at home on the Internet, they have to decide what areas of the library they need to visit. If they are researching the Challenger, they might want some photos from the newspaper on microfiche. If they have chosen Martin Luther King Jr. and want some books on their reading level, they might want to go to the Children's Literature section of the library. They evaluate their situation and come prepared to follow a strategy.

Student-Generated Criteria

By March, the children are deep into their research and are writing drafts in multiple genres. At this time I share former students' papers with them and we have a brainstorming session about how these multigenre papers should be evaluated. We do this as one large group of elementary and university students. When I asked what should be considered a good paper last year, we came up with the following:

1. Quality—Papers should be neat and have correct spelling.
2. Content—There should be lots of factual and good information included.
3. Variety of genres—There should be multiple genres included. There should be one research piece of at least two pages, a fiction or short story, three poems, and another five different genres of your choice.
4. Effort—Your paper will show effort if it makes sense and has good details.
5. Quantity—You have to write ten pieces minimum, but it would be great if you wrote more.
6. Creativity—You should include artwork, music, and color and present it in a format that is eye-catching and interesting.
7. Photos or pictures—If you include them, they should have correct captions for identification.
8. Resources—You should create a resource list of your sources to help others find your books, magazines, and Internet addresses.
9. On time—You must submit your required weekly pieces to Mrs. Swistak on time.
10. Rough drafts and revisions—You must work through the writing process. Each rough draft must be revised and complete before you begin to type it.
11. Organized—Be sure that your paper is organized, that the pieces are based upon facts, and that the pieces connect to one another.

I typed the list and distributed it to the students to place in their Resource Notebooks. It served as a reminder of what they needed to accomplish, and students knew the criteria upon which their work would be judged. This list can vary each year according to negotiations between Laurie, the children, the university students, and me.

Checklist for Multigenre Project
One of my students had the idea that a checklist of the entire multigenre project would help keep the children on track. We developed the one in Figure 10–1 based upon our brainstormed criteria for a good paper.

These checklists also go into the students' Resource Notebooks. They monitor their progress as they complete each step.

Checklist for Grading Multigenre Papers
You can discuss and refine the criteria mentioned here with your students. Jana McHenry, who is teaching the language arts methods course for me

NAME _____

I have used a variety of resources. ( )

I have a minimum of ten pieces. ( )

I have one research piece, which is 2–4 pages long. ( )

I have three poems. ( )

I have one piece of fiction or a short story. ( )

I have five pieces of my own choice. ( )

I have written and revised my rough drafts. ( )

I have written all of my pieces based on factual information. ( )

I have edited for

    grammar. ( )

    spelling. ( )

    neatness. ( )

    punctuation. ( )

    capitalization. ( )

I have included a bibliography and followed the correct
format. ( )

I have organized my paper so that each part of it relates to my
topic and connects to every other piece. ( )

I have created my paper in an interesting and eye-catching
format. ( )

I am prepared with my creative piece. ( )

I have practiced for my oral presentation and am very familiar
with my topic. ( )

FIGURE 10–1. Checklist for Multigenre Project

while I am on sabbatical and writing this book, created the following
multigenre research paper rubric (Figure 10–2) to help her holistically score
the university papers. You can see how the areas are similar to those brainstormed by the elementary and university students.

EDC 302 Multigenre Research Paper Criteria   Jana McHenry

Name:

*The final grade will be determined using the following scale:

A = exceptional completion of criteria
B = acceptable completion of criteria
C = minimal completion of criteria

   Comments:

The research paper contains multiple genres (minimum of 5) in the area of poetry, fiction, and nonfiction.	A B C
The *total number of pieces* shows dedicated effort with some longer pieces of writing.	A B C
The pieces reflect multiple *research* sources and include information derived from research, not simply pieces that could have been written without having done the research.	A B C
The *organization* reflects a systematic way of presenting the material; the pieces are tied together to form a cohesive paper.	A B C
The paper is *original/creative/moving*. There is an original way to present the information; there is something creative about it that reflects the passion that drove the project; it entices the reader to keep reading.	A B C
The *presentation* of the paper includes the arts in some form; the paper is attractive and pleasing to the eye.	A B C
There are no errors in *mechanics* with the exception of the use of Grammar B.	A B C
There are a variety of *references* cited in APA format.	A B C
The overall *quality* of the paper reflects a genuine effort on the part of the writer.	A B C
The *journal* reflects the dates and daily effort the writer engaged in to complete this project.	A B C

FIGURE 10–2.   Multigenre Research Paper Criteria

Laurie's Weekly Feedback

Each week in March and April, Laurie collects all drafts of the children's writing. She checks them for content and mechanics and returns them with suggested revisions. Students continue to revise until they meet her approval. Then she lets the children begin to type their pieces. Students know where they stand.

Laurie's Weekly Notes to Parents

Each week Laurie also sends home the following note to parents. It keeps them informed about their children's progress. This alerts parents to any potential problems and helps keep the children on track. When necessary, Laurie mails the notes to ensure parents receive them.

> Dear Parents,
>
> Our research project is progressing very nicely. I will be sending this note home on a weekly basis so that you will be informed about your child's progress.
>
> _____ has submitted _____ handwritten pieces of the required _____ for editing. If your child has not completed the rough drafts for at least _____ written pieces at this time, he/she should concentrate on completing them by _____.
>
> I am available before and after school if your child would like to meet with me.
>
> Sincerely,
>
> Mrs. Swistak

Student-generated Oral Presentation Rubrics (Chapter 9)

In April, Laurie's students watch videos of former students presenting their multigenre papers. They brainstorm criteria for a four-point rubric, which they then apply when they watch videotapes of three former students' presentations. This practice reinforces the characteristics of a strong presentation.

Peer Feedback (Chapter 9)

Also in April, Laurie's students give their oral presentations for their peers in other fifth-grade classrooms at Cranston Calvert. At this time their peers rate the presentations. This feedback from outsiders helps Laurie's children make final revisions to their oral presentations before they present at the university.

Multigenre Madness (Chapter 9)

The evening when students present at the university, they are videotaped so that they can later review their presentations. Using the Multigenre Research

Questionnaire, relatives and friends rate the students' engagement in the multigenre experience as well as their oral presentations. I photocopy the questionnaire responses and give them to Laurie to share with her students. I also share them with my students.

"About My Pieces" Page

Another helpful way for the student to reflect and for us as teachers to evaluate is for the student to create a page on which he elaborates about each piece. They can place this at the end of their multigenre papers. Laurie and I don't require this, but we offer it as a suggestion for those students who would like to try it. On this page, the student names each piece in his paper individually. Then he might comment on why he chose that particular genre, which part of the piece is based upon fact, or how the piece might be a fictional interpretation.

Interviews at Cranston Calvert

Last year, about a month after our evening of Multigenre Madness, I returned to Cranston Calvert to interview eight of Laurie's students. I asked them to respond to the following prompts:

1. Tell me about your multigenre paper.
2. Describe your relationship with your mentor.
3. Tell me about your creative arts piece.
4. Tell me about your oral presentation.
5. What did you learn through this multigenre experience?
6. What else would you like to share with me that could improve this program?

Everyone learned something different. In addition, they all had different advice for future students.

Follow-up Interviews

I also conducted a group interview with Lottie, Brian, and Julianne and then brought them back together again almost a year later. At the later interview they reinforced what they had said earlier and even compared the multigenre project favorably to what they were learning in their current class.

Reflection

The week following the oral presentations at the university, Laurie gathers her children to do a group reflection of the whole process. She asks them to brainstorm questions they might ask themselves about the whole project. She writes them on the board and the children write them in their blue books. They answer the questions for their homework. Here is what they asked last year:

1. How do you feel about your own personal project? Why do you feel this way?

2. Did you enjoy it?
3. Would you like to do a similar project?
4. Did you think it was fun to do?
5. If you could change anything, what would you change?
6. How did you choose your topic?
7. If you did another project, would you use the same topic?
8. What did you learn that you didn't know before?
9. Did you learn new skills? What?
10. Did your oral presentation go well? Explain.

Letters

For several years, Laurie and I used a letter format to get students' feedback on what they had learned from the project. Letters are informal and student responses come from the heart. Here is a letter from my student Dan about Laurie's student Adam:

Dear Mrs. Swistak,

I had a great time working with Adam. I know that it was a great learning experience for me and I think that Adam really gained from the experience as well.

Adam gained a lot of respect for the hard work that goes into writing but the most important thing that he learned is that writing really can be fun. He first discovered this with the "10 minute writes" that we worked on. I could tell that he always looked at writing as a chore instead of an enjoyable experience. When we worked on the "ten minute writes" Adam could not believe how much fun they were to do. I told Adam that he could write about anything that he wanted. Naturally, the majority of his pieces were on surfing.

Our work on poetry turned out to be the same way. Adam's first reaction to poetry was extremely negative. I think he discovered that poetry wasn't all that bad when he got to write poems about topics that interested him.

Without a doubt, Adam showed the most interest and did his best work with Hank, the fictional character that we invented. Adam enjoyed this genre so much that he asked me if he could keep writing pieces about Hank on his own throughout the week. This was the biggest success that I shared with Adam.

Adam did a lot of great work on his multigenre paper as well. It must have been hard for a fifth grader to stay focused on a subject like Jimi Hendrix. He showed a lot of imagination with some of his pieces. I think his fictitious interview was his best piece of work.

I gained a lot of confidence in my teaching skills from working with Adam. I had some trouble getting him motivated and focused on staying on task at times, however, everything always seemed to work out well. It truly was a great experience and I got more reassurance by working with Adam that I am making the right choice in choosing teaching as my profession.

Sincerely,

Dan

We also had Laurie's students write to my students to tell them what they had learned during their time together.

Dear Nicole,

I learned many things during our time together. I learned that I get more nervous than I think that I'm going to be before a speech. I learned that I tend to procrastinate when it comes to working on a report at home. I also learned that I tend to forget things before and during a report.

What I learned about research was that it's hard to find and it's even harder to organize and write a paper on. I learned that writing an interesting paper is hard. In the process I sometimes run into writer's block where I don't know what to write next or how to say something.

I learned that during a speech I need to slow down. Also, when I ask the audience a question I should give them a chance to answer it.

Thank you for all that you've taught me and for all the help you've given me in writing the report. Maybe we can get together sometime. Hope to see you soon.

Sincerely,

Lynn Marie

Post-it Notes

After the multigenre papers are complete, Laurie and I read them one final time. At this point students have done the absolute best job they can. Still, there are often some small errors that take away from the overall final presentation of their reports. At this point I do not want to write directly on their papers. I place Post-it Notes on any pages where there are errors, drawing their attention to them. I recommend that they change them because it will enhance the overall appearance of their final products. Many students choose to do so.

Laurie's Grading System

At the end of the multigenre project, Laurie grades the students in three areas. She uses the evaluation rubrics the children created as her guide. She attaches the form shown in Figure 10–3 to each paper.

My Grading System

The multigenre project constitutes one-quarter of my students' final grades. At the end of the semester, I hold a half-hour interview with each of my students during which we review the strengths and weaknesses of the entire course and discuss his or her progress in all areas. There is no way I can anticipate the insights that they will reveal. Nathan had this to offer:

> Multigenre research requires a student to build up a knowledge base and then report using his or her own creativity through multiple genres. This is probably the best way for an educator to measure a student's creativity and true understanding of researched material. With formal fact finding/recitation, students can hide their writing skills behind quotes and plagiarized material.

We review their multigenre papers and their oral presentations. It is a holistic appraisal on both our parts. They are very candid and frank with their assessments. I never give grades for the multigenre papers but rather discuss any final editing that they need to do. If they are going to use their papers as models for their future students, they need papers that are error-

---

Congratulations on a job well done.

Everyone worked very hard on the multigenre project. You have been graded in three areas. If you are unhappy about any grade, see it as an area in which you can improve.

Written multigenre paper _____

Creative piece _____

Oral presentation _____

Your wonderful imaginations shone and you learned a great deal about researching a topic.

Take these skills with you and continue to use them!

Love,
Mrs. Swistak

FIGURE 10–3. Congratulatory Note

free. I have never had a student object to not getting graded. At the end of the interview, I ask the student what grade she thinks she has earned for the course. At first students are reluctant to respond but given enough wait time, they will produce a grade. In almost every case it is a fair assessment. Having heard their perspectives on our entire course helps me understand what they have learned throughout our time together.

Thoughts on Evaluation

I think that whenever we evaluate students' work we have to keep the possible long-range effects in mind. I found Ralph Fletcher's remarks on how he speaks to students about writing very wise: "We must speak to our students with an honesty tempered by compassion: Our words will literally define the ways they perceive themselves as writers. We need to be patient: The fuse we light is a slow-burning one" (1993, 18–19).

Children are on their way to becoming literate people. We cannot expect them to know all and be able to do all by the end of this multigenre project. When we include them along the way in honest conversations about what should be acceptable criteria for teacher and self-evaluation, we help them gain a sense of responsibility for their own evaluation. We want them to learn to love literacy. We don't want to squelch that slow-burning fuse.

Now that I have brought you through our experiences with the multigenre research, I would like to summarize many of the key strategies through a series of the most commonly asked questions about multigenre research. In the next chapter you will find these questions and some suggested solutions by five teachers who have conducted multigenre research in their classrooms.

11 REFLECTIONS
*Teachers Answer Questions
About Multigenre*

For the past four years I have been writing multigenre research papers along with my students from the university. Three of those years I have worked with classroom teachers in public and private schools as they have taught multigenre research for the first time. In this final chapter, Laurie Swistak, Lesley Faria, Landa Patterson, Alison Ernest, Jana McHenry, and I would like to share our most recent thinking about multigenre research. Laurie teaches fifth grade in a public school, Lesley and Landa team teach fourth and fifth grades in a private school, Alison teaches fifth grade in a middle school, and Jana taught my university students while I was on sabbatical writing this book. Here is a compilation of our thinking. We hope this will encourage you to introduce multigenre research to your students.

Q. With which students and at what grade levels would multigenre research papers and presentations be successful?

A. Over the past four years, the teachers, my students, and I have worked with children from language arts enrichment programs, children from regular elementary classes, and special-needs students with individual education plans. Whether it is through their written pieces, their creative arts pieces, or their oral presentations, they have all found areas where they have strength and where they can be successful.

We would suggest teaching multigenre research in the fourth grade and up. Children need to be able to sustain interest in the project for a long period of time. They need to be able to read from a wide variety of resources and grasp the concept of alternate points of view. They also need to be able to analyze and synthesize material and work with a certain level of independence. Although they do not need to possess all these skills at the beginning of the project, it is among the goals of the project to develop these skills. They must have the potential to be successful in these areas. No matter at what grade level multigenre research papers are taught, the most important requirement is that students should have been writing for some time and be familiar with the writing process before you begin the project.

Q. What can I expect students to gain from writing multigenre research papers?

A. If you conduct the multigenre project the way we have discussed in this book, you can be sure that the following knowledge and skills will be addressed.

Students learn to:
conduct library and Internet research
read analytically from a variety of sources
write and revise in multiple genres for multiple purposes
monitor their progress through journal writing
speak in small groups
speak before large groups
listen to peers
critique peers
self-evaluate
use technology (Internet, word processing, application programs)
think and problem solve with peers and independently
think creatively by integrating the arts with their research
organize their time
collaborate with others inside and outside the classroom

Q. Where should I begin?

A. You need to see how this project fits into your existing school year plan. First review any state standards and school curriculum requirements. Cross tab these and generate a list of all the areas and skills you need to accomplish for the year. Determine your time constraints and set a project schedule. It works best if you can integrate the multigenre research paper with your existing curriculum. This integration will affect your students' freedom of topic selection and the number and types of genres that will be required.

Although it is best to introduce the multigenre research paper in the last half to third of the year, it is important to make your students aware of it early in the fall. Get them thinking about areas of interest. Put together a book of samples of plays, short stories, essays, interviews, newspaper articles, and poetry for their reference.

Also, it is very helpful to get your students writing and editing before you actually introduce the multigenre paper. They should write four or five times a week, practice selecting their own topics to write about, and have the chance to get responses to their writing from you and their classmates. Getting used to writing response journals will also ease them into self-evaluation. Lastly, it would be helpful if they had the chance to interview one another or other teachers or children in the building. All these skills are not prerequisite but having developed some of them will make the transition into the multigenre papers a bit easier.

Q. How much time should I dedicate to a multigenre project?

A. This will depend upon what you are trying to accomplish for the year and how you structure your class time. We like using three months in the spring because what we try to accomplish builds on prerequisite skills learned in the fall and winter.

We like three months because we think that children need to work for a sustained period of time. They have to accomplish so much with this project and we don't want to rush them. It takes time to choose topics, practice various genres, construct rubrics, write reflections, and pull the whole project together.

We also like that time period because there are two weeklong vacations during the project. The first week off comes after their practice with poetry, character sketches, and nonfiction. By this time, they have also chosen topics and completed their K–W–Ls. Over the break they have time to generate more questions and think about the forms of writing they are going to use. The second vacation week comes near the end of the project when they have to complete their creative arts pieces and practice for their oral presentations. When they return from the second vacation week, they have one more meeting to rehearse their entire presentations and then they go to the university to present.

Having the project span three months also helps students learn organizational and time-management skills. It reinforces the idea that anything worth doing takes time and hard work.

Q. How can I help students choose their topics?

A. First you have to decide how much freedom you are going to allow for student choice. Complete freedom without guidelines sometimes is overwhelming for students. It can cause students to choose topics about which they are not passionate. They choose more on a whim because they lack direction. It is best to focus upon a person or an event. You might want to limit the topics to integrate with a theme you are studying, such as the Renaissance.

Once you have set your overall guidelines you can help students by sharing topics that former students have chosen. There is a list of these in Chapter 3. Give students time to discuss topic choice in small groups and brainstorm additional topics as possibilities. Have them talk about people they admire or occupations they might want to pursue and the people who are outstanding in those fields. Bring in newspapers and newsmagazines and have them discuss current events. Discuss a general time line of the last century and some of the key events that have taken place. Since it was the millennium, for the last set of multigenre papers, the teachers suggested that their students choose people or events from the last one hundred years. Be careful about very recent events because students might be limited to Internet resources. We want students to become familiar with more than technological references. You might also consider the resources you can make available in the classroom. It is sometimes difficult for some children to get to their local libraries and they might have little parent support at home. So you might have to limit topic selection to choices for which resources would be available within your school.

Encourage children to talk to their friends and family members about choices. Many times, students have selected topics after discussions around the dinner table. The key point in topic selection is *choice*. If students don't choose their own topics, they will lack commitment. It is too big a project to spend three months researching and writing about something that is boring.

This brings up another point. If a student does choose a topic and after researching it, she finds that she really has no emotional involvement with it, it is best to abandon the topic and search for something more meaningful. It will be well worth the additional investment in time. You will have to decide, however, a deadline after which students will not be allowed to change their topics. That is why it is good to work with students for at least a month before they actually have to choose their topics.

Q. How long should multigenre papers be?

A. Teachers and students should determine the length of the multigenre papers together. This will partially be determined by grade level. The older the students, the more pieces should be considered. Laurie requires a two- to four-page expository research piece. This helps students develop skill in writing a traditional research report. She also requires either a piece of fiction or a newspaper piece that gives students the chance to write connected text in a more creative way. A third genre that she requires is poetry. Because there are so many forms of poetry, she usually allows students to include more than one type. The remaining pieces are of the students' choice. All together, Laurie requires a minimum of ten pieces. Alison and her students have negotiated for nine pieces. Above that would exceed her required standard. Landa and Lesley want their students to write fewer but longer pieces for their multigenre papers. They require four pieces: a piece of nonfiction; a fictional piece, which could be a play, a short story, or an interview; a piece of poetry; and a time line. Jana believes that substance is more important than the length of multigenre papers. She finds that most students write more than is required as enthusiasm for their projects builds.

Q. How should I manage the writing and revision of the paper?

A. Once teachers and students decide on the required genres and the minimum number of free-choice pieces that students should incorporate into their papers, teachers need to impose weekly deadlines. This can be accomplished by completing a weekly assignment or goal-setting sheet for each student or by giving them a schedule of due dates at the beginning of the project.

Laurie requires that her students complete the two- to four-page research pieces first. This forces them to read, analyze, and synthesize the information that sets the background for all pieces in their papers. Starting with that piece, she begins a weekly revision cycle during which she reads and gives students feedback on each piece of their writing. Landa and Lesley place more emphasis on self-editing and peer editing before students submit their papers to the teachers for revision. Alison gives her students an editing check sheet that requires at least two peers to edit each piece of writing. She reviews these and then bases her next whole-group language arts lesson on common errors that she has found. She asks students to look specifically for those errors the next time they are editing.

In addition, Laurie sends weekly notes home to parents letting them know how many pieces students have completed and what they need to be working on next. Parents help monitor student progress and revision at home. This keeps the project moving forward.

This weekly cycle helps students realize that although they will be given the time to revise, they must eventually be responsible to meet a deadline. As the project progresses, students get better at meeting deadlines, writing, and editing. They begin to internalize these skills.

Q. Are oral presentations necessary to the multigenre projects? If so, how should I manage them?

A. Yes, we feel the oral presentation is a critical component of the multigenre project because it serves many purposes. First, it helps students develop oral communication skills and build confidence in themselves as public speakers. It also serves as a vehicle for students to introduce themselves, explain why they chose their topics, build background information for their listeners, and read many of their written pieces. Student oral presentations also build the connection between their papers and their creative arts pieces.

The length of time you should dedicate to these oral presentations will depend upon the number of students in your class and the amount of time you can spare for this production. We allow students five to seven minutes each. If the presentations are too long, they will lose the audience's interest. We hold no more than five or six presentations at one sitting. This allows time for transitions between students and time for peer evaluation. You can have students present over a period of days or run concurrent small-group presentations so students can all finish their presentations in about an hour, as we do.

Q. How and when do I assess this project?

A. It is important to assess throughout the project. Constant feedback is necessary because so much of the project must be accomplished independently. It is also important to include students in the design of the assessment and to give them responsibility for self-assessment. Over the years, we have used the following means to help us with our assessment:

pre and post literacy and attitude assessments
response journals
teacher evaluation of student notebooks and note cards
student-generated rubrics for multigenre papers and presentations
self-editing
peer editing
teacher conferences
peer critiques of oral presentations
self-critiques of oral presentations
parent feedback on entire project
videotaped student practice of oral presentations with reflections
weekly goal-setting assignment sheets
student-generated K–W–L charts
overall checklists for multigenre papers and presentations
weekly teacher notes to parents
student interviews
student final reflection letters to the teacher

These forms of assessment take into account students' written, oral, and performance work. There are no tests associated with this project. Tests would be not be appropriate in such a performance-based learning situation. Final grading should involve conferencing and narrative comments rather than a simple A, B, or C grade.

Q. How important is parent or volunteer involvement in this project?

A. Multigenre projects can be done without the use of parent or volunteer involvement in the classroom. It is good to communicate with parents, however, and to keep them informed about their children's progress. Laurie sends home a letter about a month before the project begins. She gives the parents an overview of what is to come and also tells them that she will be in communication with them throughout. As soon as the children choose their topics, she lets the parents know about them and asks that if they have or know of any resources that might help any of the children in the class to please send either the resources or information to her. Then she sends a weekly note home informing parents of the progress of their children. Toward the end of the project, she tells them when and where the Multigenre Madness night will take place and asks for their help with videotaping the presentations and baking refreshments. At the end of the presentations, parents are also asked for their input on the whole experience.

Overall, parents tend to help the most with the artistic component of the project. They can also be most helpful in taking their children to the local libraries to help them find books and materials for their research.

If you would like to get parents and/or other volunteers involved in the classroom, it would be very helpful to hold an introductory meeting where you would explain the multigenre project. Then you should hold several workshops to teach volunteers about the writing and editing process. You could then schedule two or three volunteers for several hours a week to help the children with their papers. To be effective, these volunteers must respect student choice and learn to facilitate rather than dictate.

Q. What can a teacher expect to gain from teaching a multigenre research paper to students?

A. You gain a strong sense of satisfaction from knowing that what you are teaching is important. It has value for your students. In addition to language arts skills, students gain in areas that are difficult to measure but are so important for their success in the real world.

Students Change and Grow
I have worked closely enough with elementary and university students over the past four years to have witnessed how multigenre research has made a difference to them. It has changed them.

Students Become More Interested in Content
Students learn to delve deeply into areas that interest them. Students see themselves and their peers become emotionally attached to topics. These topics become important. They are varied and interesting. Students want to hear what their peers have to say. They not only read one another's papers and listen to one another's final presentations but also discuss these topics throughout the project. They peer edit and critique as well as discuss their research in and outside of class. Learning content in this way is much more interesting than learning it from a text—and they remember it.

Students Gain a New Attitude Toward Learning
From the start, students make choices about topics and genres. They constantly talk among themselves about what's important and how they can

make others understand. They are actively involved in every aspect of the project. They see what others before them have accomplished and they want to do as much or more. Reluctant writers turn into avid writers. Students take risks through the creative and performing arts. They are not passive receptors of instruction. They show initiative. They take charge of their learning.

Students Build Self-Confidence

Because they must take charge of their learning, students must look closely at how they are doing. They spend time reflecting in response journals, evaluating themselves, and evaluating one another. They begin to see value in what they and their peers are accomplishing. They test ideas on peers. They applaud final products. Parents applaud, too. Shy students step forward and shine. You see passion in their eyes and hear it in their voices. Classmates grow to know and appreciate one another. They also appreciate themselves. Students' self-confidence soars.

Students Learn to Think

Multigenre research demands that students communicate. They question how they will write and present their information. They question, problem solve, and try to decide whether or not it is going well and what their options are. They openly and honestly discuss issues about their topics, their writing, and their desire to do well. They demonstrate unusual focus. They lose sense of time and think about the papers when not working on them. They're in a constant state of composing.

Teachers Change and Grow

In addition to seeing my students grow and change in so many ways, I have found that engagement with multigenre research has changed me as a teacher, too.

Teachers Learn About Modeling

Writing my own multigenre paper each year pushes me to serve as a model for my students. I continue to develop my own writing skills. I continue to learn how to share my thinking strategies about the whole process. I have to stretch myself to incorporate the fine or performing arts, and I have to choose new areas to investigate. I see each year what it's like to meet deadlines and complete assignments. I learn better ways to talk about my frustrations and successes with research, writing, and presenting with my students.

Teachers Learn About the World

I learn a lot about my students' worlds and the world in general. They select topics I would not necessarily choose and they open my mind to new avenues of exploration. I remember each and every topic that former students have written and spoken about because we lived through the process together.

I've learned about musicians, historical figures, artists, sports, current events, and topics of personal interest to my students. Because I associate the topics with my students, I remember their faces and the creative ways they presented them, and I remember the content.

Teachers Learn About Teaching

Working side by side on multigenre papers with my students helps me know them as people. I see how they learn, what motivates them, and what excites them. I use this knowledge to help myself become a better teacher in the future. I've learned to be a facilitator and manager of independent and meaningful projects, all different and all OK.

Teachers Learn to Expect the Unexpected

When I first introduced multigenre to my students, I had no idea how it would go. I was much like you probably are now, wondering whether or not it is worth the risk. I took the chance. I redesigned my entire teaching language arts methods course to center around this paper. I fully integrated it with my existing curriculum and used the multigenre paper as a vehicle to teach everything I wanted my students to be able to teach when they would become teachers of language arts. It has been a challenge, but it keeps my learning fresh and flexible. Over the past four years I have continued to modify requirements for the paper and presentation as I have learned new things. Each year student papers and presentations become better and better as we learn from previous experiments. I have learned to build and negotiate curriculum and to always be prepared to change.

Q. What words of advice would you offer to a teacher who is trying multigenre research for the first time?

A. Be prepared to be constantly surprised by your students as they push beyond your wildest expectations. Be prepared to become emotionally involved with them as they engulf you with their beautifully expressive writing and a fresh sense of wonder about the world. Be grateful that you have the chance to introduce them to a love of learning that you didn't expect was possible.

Appendix

My Sacajawea Report
An Example of a Multigenre Paper

My Sacajawea Report

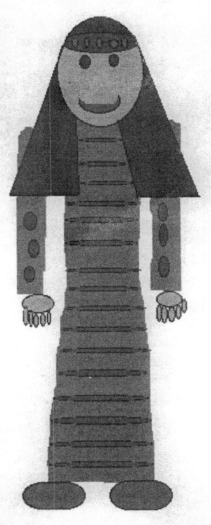

By: Claudia Rotondo

Claudia Rotondo

My Sacajawea Report

Sacajawea was born in 1787. She was from the Shoshoni tribe in Idaho. At the time of her birth her name was Huichu. At age 11 her people were attacked by the Hidatsa warriors. They changed her name to Sacajawea. There are three ways to spell Sacajawea. They are Sacajawea, Sacagawea and Sakakawea.

After she had lived with the Hidatsa Indians for five years, a man named Toussaint Charbonneau bought her from the Hidatsa chief. Sacajawea became his wife at age sixteen. At age seventeen Sacajawea had a son named Jean Baptiste, nicked named Pomp which means first born.

In 1804 Charbonneau was asked by Lewis & Clark to join the westward expedition and to serve as a interpreter. Sacajaewa was asked to come along also to communicate different languages. Their goal was to reach the Pacific Ocean.

By April 7, 1805, the expedition had moved along the

Missouri River west to the mountains.

By August 15,1805, Sacajawea was reunited with her old tribe the Shoshonis. She discovered that her whole family had died except two of her brothers and the son of her oldest sister.

Her brother Caneahwait was chief of the Shoshoni tribe. He sketched a map of the west and provided a guide, Old Toby, to help the expedition. The expedition ended in the summer of 1806. They had reached their goal, the Pacific Ocean. Sacajawea, Charbonneau and Jean Baptiste returned home to Fort Mandan in the Dakotas. Captain Clark sent them a letter and asked them to come to St.Louis or they could send Jean Baptiste to Clark so he could educate him.

Sacajawea, Charbonneau and Jean Baptiste moved to St. Louis. In March 1811 Sacajawea and Charbonneau moved back to the Dakotas. Jean Baptiste remained in St. Louis with Clark for his education.

There are two storys about Sacajaweas death. The first one says that Sacajawea died on December 20, 1812 of a

fever at age 25. This information was found in written documents from this time period. The other story is a legend that has been passed down. This one says she died on April 9, 1884 of old age.

Many people, including me, tend to believe the first story that she died at age 25 because there is written proof, where the other story is just a legend.

Forests were dark and spooky
Streams babbling
Rivers rushing
Beautiful sunsets and
Harsh weather

The nights were dark and gloomy
The days were bright from the sun
Dusk came too soon

I can hear the animals howling,sends a chill down my back
The streams are babbling underneath the canoe
The wind is whistling in my ears
I hear birds singing lovely songs

Where are we going?
How long will it be?
Will we meet any Indians?

I feel scared and
And anxious and
Excited about the juorney

Scared
Scared
Scared

S–taying with the Lewis and Clark expedition

A–t age 11 she was captured by the Hidatsa Indians

C–aring for her baby Jean Baptiste

A–fter 5 years of living with the Hidatsa Tribe, Sacajawea married Charbonneau

J–ourneying through the west, she served as a communicator

A–fter months of traveling she is reunited with her old tribe

W–ith her family she traveled west to reach their destination

E–xpediton ended in 1806

A–ll lived happily until her death in 1812

I am an Indian
I am a mother
I am a wife
I am a wilderness guide
I am a girl
I am a sister
I am a mother
I am Sacajawea

Once there was an Indian girl, Sacajawea

Who loved to ride in her Kia

This is a lie of course

She rode only a horse

This is too hard, I should write an Onamonapia!!!

Obituary

Sacajawea was born in 1787 to the Shoshoni Indian Tribe. She spent a portion of her life living with the Hidatsa Indian Tribe because at age 11, her tribe (the Shoshoni's) were attacked by the Hidatsa Warriors. They captured her and made her a slave.

She was married to a French-Canadian Fur Trader named Toussaint Charbonneau. At age 17 Sacajawea had a son. She named him Jean Baptiste.

With Jean on her back and Charbonneau serving as a interpreter, they all helped two men named Lewis and Clark. She helped them reach their destination, the Pacific Ocean. The Lewis and Clark expedition ended in the summer of 1806. Sacajawea died at age 25 on the 20th of December, 1812 in Fort Manual, South Dakota.

Besides her husband, Toussaint Chrbonneau, she leaves behind a son, Jean Baptiste. Her son now lives in St. Louis, Missouri.

Fiction

"Sacajawea's DEAD!!!" Everyone in the village of the Shoshoni tribe was screaming and yelling. The Hidatsa warriors thought they had killed Sacajawea and William Clark.

Sacajawea and Clark had really run away, badly injured. They weren't dead. They escaped without telling anyone.

When they reached safety, Sacajawea and Clark believed they were somewhere in Virginia.

There was nobody around to help them, so Sacajawea had to use her skills on how to heal wounds.

After a year of living together, they decided to get married. Two years later, they had a son. They named him John. Soon they had another son named David. One year after John's birth, Sacajawea delivered a daughter. They named her Mary.

They found a old, battered farm just outside of Williamsburg, Virginia. They cleaned it and spent many happy years there. Sacajawea, Clark, David, John and Mary all lived a happy life and the legend is true, she died on April 9, 1884 of old age. Clark spent his remaining years as a farmer on their farm, just outside of Williamsburg, Virginia.

JOIN THE EXPEDITION!!!

LEWIS & CLARK
ARE GOING WEST
IF YOU WOULD LIKE TO
JOIN, YOU MUST BE BRAVE,
ADVENTUROUS AND HAVE
WILDERNESS SKILLS.
YOU ALSO MUST BE STRONG
SIGN UP NOW THE
GENERAL STORE, ST. CHARLES, MO.
MUST HAVE OWN GEAR
LEAVING ON
MAY 21, 1804
AT 7:00 AM SHARP!!!

Dear Diary,   April 7, 1805

Today we continued our journey with Meriwether Lewis an William Clark. I worry that Jean Baptiste will will not fare well on such a long journey. Jean Baptiste enjoyed the fresh air.

Today we moved along the Missouri River, west of the mountains. We saw many deer. One of the hunters shot one for supper tonight while I collected roots to eat. Toussaint says that if we keep up at this pace, we will be at the Pacific before summer begins. I do not believe him. Well, I am very tired. I must rest. Tomorrow we have much to do and many miles to travel.

Dear Diary,   August 15, 1805

Today I was reunited with my tribe, the Shoshonis. I was sad to hear that my whole family had died except two of my brothers and the son of my oldest sister. I happy to hear that brother Caneahwait, is now chief of the tribe. He will make a great leader. Caneahwait gave us a map and a guide, Old Toby. I hope this helps the expedition go faster.Part of me wants to stay with my tribe, but I must continue with the expedition.

The Boston Herald

March 17, 1805

Fort Mandan, Dakota Territory-This morning the Meriwether Lewis and William Clark expedition continued their journey west to the Pacific ocean. They are traveling North and West of the Missouri River. They will receive help from a Shoshoni Indian girl named Sacajawea. She agreed to help the explorers. Her husband, Toussaint Charbonneau, will serve as a interpreter.

Lewis and Clark hired Sacajawea to speak different Indian Languages, to get horses and to help lead the way to the Pacific Ocean.

President Jefferson conceived of an expedition to explore the Louisiana Territory. They will travel along the Missouri River, west of the mountains.

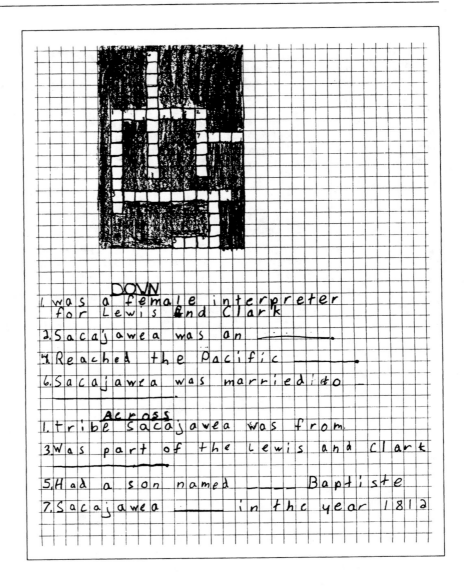

DOWN

1. was a female interpreter for Lewis and Clark

2. Sacajawea was an _____

4. Reached the Pacific _____

6. Sacajawea was married to _____

Across

1. tribe Sacajawea was from

3. Was part of the Lewis and Clark _____

5. Had a son named _____ Baptiste

7. Sacajawea _____ in the year 1812

Bibliography

1. http://lewisandclark.org
2. http://www.rootsweb.com/~nwa/Sacajawea.html
3. http://www.teacherlink.usu.edu/resources/ed lesson plans/famous/sacajawe.html
4. http://www.teleport.com/~megaines/sacajawea.htm
5. http://www.bostonherald.com/bostonherald/nat/07saca.htm
6. http://www.3.org/weta/thewest/wpages/wpgs400w4sacaga.htm
7. http://www.letsfindout.com/america/sacagawe.html

1.Sacajawea
Virginia Frances Voight
G.P. Putnam's sons
New York
©1967

2.Sacajawea, Wilderness Guide
Kate Jassem
Troll Associates
©1979

3.Undaunted Courage
Steven E. Ambrose
Simon & Shuster
New York
©1996

References

Andrea Bocelli: A Night in Tuscany. 1997. PolyGram Video, a division of PolyGram Records, Inc., New York, New York.

Birdwell, N. 1985. *Clifford Gets a Job.* New York: Scholastic Trade.

Cameron, J. 1998. *The Right to Write: An Invitation and Initiation into the Writing Life.* New York: Tarcher/Putnam.

Chaney, A., and T. Burk. 1998. *Teaching Oral Communication in Grades K–8.* Needham Heights, MA: Allyn and Bacon.

Csikszentmihalyi, M. 1990. *Flow: The Psychology of Optimal Experience.* New York: Harper & Row.

Edwards, B. 1999. *Drawing on the Right Side of the Brain.* New York: Penguin Putnam Inc.

Fletcher, R. 1993. *What a Writer Needs.* Portsmouth, NH: Heinemann.

Goleman, D. 1995. *Emotional Intelligence.* New York: Bantam Books.

Graves, D. 1999. *Bring Life into Learning.* Portsmouth, NH: Heinemann.

———. 1992. *Explore Poetry.* Portsmouth, NH: Heinemann.

Hansen, J. 1998. *When Learners Evaluate.* Portsmouth, NH: Heinemann.

Heard, G. 1999. *Awakening the Heart.* Portsmouth, NH: Heinemann.

———. 1995. *Writing Toward Home.* Portsmouth, NH: Heinemann.

McCourt, F. 1996. *Angela's Ashes.* New York: Scribner's.

McCullough, D. 1999. *Paris Review* 152 (Fall).

National Council of Teachers of English (NCTE) and the International Reading Association (IRA). 1996. *Standards for the English Language Arts.*

Owston, R. 1998. *Making the Link: Teacher Professional Development on the Internet.* Portsmouth, NH: Heinemann.

Rogovin, P. 1998. *Classroom Interviews.* Portsmouth, NH: Heinemann.

Romano, T. 2000. *Blending Genre, Altering Style.* Portsmouth, NH: Boynton/Cook.

———. 1995. *Writing with Passion.* Portsmouth, NH: Boynton/Cook.

Scollon, R., and S. Scollon. 1986. "The Axe Handle Academy: A Proposal for a Bioregional, Thematic, Humanities Education" (Commissioned Paper). Juneau, AK: Sealaska Heritage Foundation.

Sylwester, R. 1998. "Art for the Brain's Sake." *Educational Leadership* 56 (3): 31–35.

———. 1994. "How Emotions Affect Learning." *Educational Leadership* 52 (2): 60–65.

White, B. 1995. *Mama Makes Up Her Mind: And Other Dangers of Southern Living.* Reading, MA: Addison-Wesley.

Wilhelm, J. D., and B. Edmiston. 1998. *Imagining to Learn.* Portsmouth, NH: Heinemann.